They Rise Like A Wave
An Anthology of Asian American Women Poets

They Rise Like A Wave
An Anthology of Asian American Women Poets

EDITED BY

CHRISTINE KITANO AND ALYCIA PIRMOHAMED

Blue Oak Press
Rocklin | California

Cover Design by Maxima Kahn
Cover Photograph by Jennifer Wu
Typeset in Adobe Jenson Pro

Printed and bound by Bookmobile
Printed in the United States

Library of Congress Cataloging-in-Publication Data
White, Randy
They Rise Like A Wave:
An Anthology of Asian American Women Poets
Edited by Christine Kitano and Alycia Pirmohamed

ISBN 978-0-9975040-3-3

To the future generations
of Asian American poets and writers

CONTENTS

Introduction

The impetus for *They Rise Like a Wave* came from the results of the 2016 U.S. presidential election, which smashed any idealistic notions we may have held about a shared vision of democracy among ourselves and our communities. The past several years have seen the systematic dismantling of laws, rights, and protections, laying bare the hard truth that North America has never been the mythic melting pot, the land of equal opportunity. We must also acknowledge that the vision of North America as a political and cultural entity is itself founded on the on-going occupation of Indigenous lands. The delusional logic of white supremacy underwrites these myths, often masquerading under con-cepts of individualism, boot strapping, and the "American dream." Of course, nothing about this is new. History's cyclical menace plants us in the middle of a generations-long conflict.

At a time when institutional policies have sought to silence, marginalize, deport, or otherwise erase the existences of women of color, we have never been less silent. This anthology aims to capture the voices of Asian American women and non-binary poets writing through this moment. Our contributors range from established poets who are widely published, such as Marilyn Chin and Bhanu Kapil, to emerging voices who we are excited to see more published work from in the coming years. When compiling any anthology, common reso-nances undoubtedly emerge—many of the poems in *They Rise Like a Wave*, for example, make use of the personal lyric "I" and are written in free verse. Many of the poems also navigate narratives about immigra-tion, languages, food, and other topics that are often associated with an Asian American poetics. Often intersecting with these broader top-ics are other personal and political themes—gestures toward the natu-ral world, climate grief, modern mythological retellings, and homages to loved ones—to name only a few. In our selections, we endeavor to show that there is no single style, topic, or theme that defines an Asian American poetics. More than looking for commonalities among the poems, we invite readers to attune themselves to how each poem provides a unique response to this world in this moment.

Though editorial preference is unavoidable, and we are both poets of the academy, we aim to resist reinforcing establishment values of "good" poetry, but instead to present a sampling of the range of styles, forms, and traditions that constitute an Asian American poetics at this moment in time. We often considered how we'd bring these poems into our classrooms: which poems would prove both delightful and instructive to this upcoming generation of writers, readers, and scholars? If we have an explicit metric of value it is this—a poem should defy or challenge easy categorization, even when chosen for inclusion in an anthology whose structural directive would seem to demand a coherent if not singular vision. *They Rise Like a Wave* is an anthology that captures the dynamic and shifting landscape of Asian American poetry, a poetics that continues to grow and transform, a poetics that continues by breaking boundaries, experimenting with language, and revitalizing a historically narrow and oppressive Western canon. These poems emerge out of this particular political and historical moment—a time when language's challenge to represent the complexities of reality is an aesthetic, political, and moral charge.

In this time of heightened political and cultural conflict, a time defined by increased binary oppositions between who does and does not belong, there is the simultaneous flourishing of Asian American poetry, especially poetry by women and non-binary writers. This is made possible in part by increased access to literary resources, both in the academy and in community-based organizations. We are grateful to independent magazines and online mediums, which have always been first to champion the work of underrepresented writers. While we see the increase of creative writing programs at both the undergraduate and graduate levels, we also see more community-based programs such as Kundiman, VONA, and the Kearny Street Workshop: spaces dedicated to nurturing the next generation of artists of color. Furthermore, the internet offers more democratized access to publishing platforms; in addition to the *Asian American Literary Review, Hyphen, Kartika, Lantern Review, Rungh Magazine,* and the Asian American Writers' Workshop's *The Margins,* new online journals like *Bitter Melon* provide dedicated publication space to young, underrepresented voices. Asian American poetry begins also to enter larger cultural institutions; the Smithsonian Asian Pacific America Center hosted the now biannual Asian American Literature Festival for the first time in Washington, D.C. in 2017; in 2018, both Diana Khoi Nguyen's *Ghost Of* and Jenny Xie's *Eye Level* were finalists for the National Book Award, Doyali Islam's *heft* was a finalist for the Griffin Poetry Prize in 2020, and in 2021, Mei-mei Berssenbrugge's *A Treatise on Stars* was a finalist for the Pulitzer Prize.

Our anthology builds upon the groundbreaking work of others. The *Aiiieeee!* anthology (1974), of course, is the first anthology of its kind, showcasing the work of Chinese American and Japanese American fiction writers. This work gives rise to anthologies that expand the scope of Asian American literature, especially in the realm of poetry; notable milestones include Garrett Hongo's *The Open Boat: Poems from Asian America* (1993), Juliana Chang's *Quiet Fire: A Historical Anthology of Asian American Poetry 1892-1970* (1996), Victoria Chang's *Asian American Poetry: The Next Generation* (2004), Neelanjana Banerjee, Summi Kaipa, and Pireeni Sundaralingam's *Indivisible: An Anthology of Contemporary South Asian American Poetry* (2010), and more recently, the ambitious *To Gather Your Leaving: Asian Diaspora Poetry from America, Australia, UK and Europe,* edited by Boey Kim Cheng, Arin Alycia Fong and Justin Chia (2019). The past fifteen years have also seen a growing number of scholarly studies devoted to Asian American poetry, among them Xiaojing Zhou's *The Ethics and Poetics of Alterity in Asian American Poetry* (2006), Steven Yao's *Foreign Acts: Chinese American Verse from Exclusion to Post-Ethnicity* (2010), Dorothy Wang's *Thinking Its Presence: Form, Race, and Subjectivity in Contemporary Asian American Poetry* (2013), and Timothy Yu's *Race and the Avant-Garde: Experimental and Asian American Poetry Since 1965* (2009) and *Nests and Strangers: On Asian American Women Poets* (2015). These works provide the opportunity to re-examine Asian American poetry as a multivalent tradition as well as to introduce new voices and perspectives. We hope *They Rise Like a Wave* serves as an invitation to further conversation, as another way station on this ongoing journey.

An anthology is always a time capsule, a reflection of the moment in which it is compiled. We began collecting poems in late 2018 and were finalizing our vision by late 2019. And then, the world shifted under our feet. The COVID-19 pandemic hit North America in full force by March 2020, closing schools and businesses and mandating stay-at-home orders. Early reports identified a market in Wuhan, China as the epicenter of the virus and across the globe, Asians and Asian Americans faced blame for the pandemic. President Trump's insistence on calling it the "Chinese virus" fueled bigoted acts of aggression against Asians and Asian Americans. And then, on May 25, 2020, George Floyd, a Black American man, was murdered by a white police officer in Minnesota, sparking outrage and protests, not just in the Americas, but across the globe.

We were closing out our work on the anthology in January 2021 when the United States witnessed a mob's assault on the Capitol, an attempted coup, prompted and falsely justified by claims of a stolen election. Despite these efforts to derail the democratic process, the United States successfully inaugurated President Joseph Biden as the 46th president, along with Vice President Kamala Harris, the first woman to hold this office, a woman of both Black and Asian American descent. Still, there is the continued violence against Asians and Asian Americans, which is just the latest evolution of anti-Asian sentiment in North America. The murders of eight people at spas in Atlanta, Georgia in March 2021, six of whom were women of Asian descent, make devastatingly clear that the dehumanizing intersection of racialized and sexualized rhetoric can be lethal.

It's been a difficult few years, but at this time of reckoning and renewal, let us remember that poetry can be both a reflection of lived experience as well as a call to imagine how to build a better world. President Biden's inauguration featured National Youth Poet Laureate Amanda Gorman, who read from "The Hill We Climb," reminding us that "Somehow we've weathered and witnessed a nation that isn't broken, but simply unfinished." Her reading has ushered in renewed attention on poetry's role as a real social and political force.

We hope the poems in this anthology offer both an artifact of this time as well as a way forward as we continue the work of envisioning and making a more just world.

Christine Kitano and Alycia Pirmohamed
January, 2022

Foreword by Sandeep Parmar

What does it mean to be Asian American, to be an Asian American poet writing today? Let us sit with these terms and their magnetism, the contracting tension between words that draw across regions, countries, histories of migration, and a tradition in English founded on the testimonies of whiteness. Let us add to this the specificities of gender—of women and non-binary people—and call to mind without inhibition the pooling expectations around identities that have drawn and redrawn themselves with increasing frequency over the recent past. As the editors of this anthology detail in their introduction, the last four or five years offer a stinging reply: to be Asian in North America amid the political upheavals of an anti-immigrant US administration, the pandemic, rising xenophobia and its attendant violence (not in itself new but transformed by Covid-19) is to become visible where there had sometimes been a safe proximity to whiteness. In her acclaimed book, *Minor Feelings*, Cathy Park Hong explains the microaggressions unique to assumptions about certain Asian Americans: we are the model minority who "'inhabit a vague purgatorial status' among races as desperately assimilating into a predominately white society that sees us as useful but without 'inner resources.'" The oppression of Asians by the US government in the twentieth-century across global imperial invasions and brutal laws at home adds some dimension to the relationship different Asian migrant groups have with their adopted country. What we find in the poems here is a working through of those histories—personal and political—as they interfere with belonging to a national imaginary. Herein the spectrum of Asian identity is strikingly dissimilar and yet familiar all the same whether as inheritors of trauma from the Korean and Vietnam wars, of India's Partition, or Asian refugee populations or economic migrants: war and displacement haunt intergenerationally to destabilize poem after poem from established writers and emerging ones alike. As Mary-Kim Arnold writes in "Forgotten War," "Is it useful to ask / who is the enemy or where do I belong." And while there is no Asian American "content," no set of subjects neatly ordained as such, what is striking is the recurrence of the aforementioned tension—to write as an Asian American poet is almost a tense of its own: past, future and present merging to form a language held in the twilight of remembering which is forgetting. What emerges are distinctive voices that each challenge a linguistic silence brought about by the condition of a racial positioning that is, in North America, still wide, uncertain, questioning itself and unfixing itself in ways that perhaps no other racial identity as broad as this does. As Celina Su so aptly puts it "A dispersal is not / a diaspora but / a population-wide tearing of limbs." In the poetic sense, the limbs of Orpheus (or Osiris) constitute a severing of a mournable body that is the poem's lyric voice. The trope of scattering and a failure to account for or bury—to make meaningful, to lay in the ground, to make fertile again—our ancestors is a longstanding pain that permeates many of the poems in this anthology through lyric tension. Gathering what one can find of one's own story is its own kind of violence possibly, but it is a necessary one. And as so many daughter personae inform us throughout this anthology—sometimes ambivalently—that, as Kate Hao puts it, "To inherit is to combust."

They Rise Like a Wave does indeed have a tidal momentum, the quick succession of many poets' voices in short selection is an invitation for readers to seek out further work by new and established poets from Marilyn Chin to Bhanu Kapil to Victoria Chang. As the anthology's editors note, this book comes at a time of great flowering and terrible upheaval, and the poems attest to a newfound energy and access offered by arts organizations, mentorship programs, fellowships, academic communities and, not least, a burgeoning readership galvanized by social change. A variety of forms—among these the villanelle, ghazal, haibun—and experimental, syntactically rich innovative poems abound within these pages: the short, tight lines of Swati Rana, the starkly visual obituary columns of Victoria Chang, Jennifer S. Cheng's epistles, the collapsed lineations of Franny Choi. Elsewhere an archival instinct is evident in Carlina Duan's poems which engage with the materiality of historical sources, namely the Chinese Exclusion Act of 1882. The presumed universality of the lyric speaker and its accompanying exoticising of the non-white body appears here throughout, from Eileen R. Tabios's Ashbery "Riff-Offs" to Alyssa Ogi's ecocritical rejoinder to Romanticism: "A mentor says my poetry is too preoccupied with race. There is / nothing timeless about sensationalism, and he quotes Coleridge / as if Coleridge parroted the words of God. He tells me to / examine pine trees for wisdom." Asian American poetry exists across the fissures between what it means to be any of these things in a world increasingly preoccupied with race and racism. And if there is one thing that anthologies like this can do—beyond move readers to expand their field of vision—it is to pay witness to these new possibilities of being and of language forming, yes, like waves, coming fast and faster towards us on the horizon.

Jessica Abughattas

Jessica Abughattas is a poet of Palestinian heritage, born and raised in California. Her debut poetry collection, *Strip* (University of Arkansas Press), won the 2020 Etel Adnan Poetry Prize, selected by Fady Joudah and Hayan Charara, who noted, "*Strip* is a captivating debut about desire and dispossession, and that tireless poetic metaphor, the body. Audacious and clear-eyed, plainspoken and brassy, these are songs that break free from confinement." She is a Kundiman fellow and a graduate of the Antioch University Los Angeles MFA in Creative Writing program. Her poems appear in *Waxwing*, *The Adroit Journal*, *Redivider*, and other places.

The Wedding

We dressed your mother when the roads
reopened. The women draped
a black cloak over her shoulders
until she was safe inside. The church
lit up like a jack o' lantern. The boys
rubbed their faces with onions, inhaled
deep to clear the fumes from the gunfire.
Souls turned over
in their graves. Your parents
married All Hallows' Eve while it rained
bullets over the minarets. No reception
but your grandfather may he rest in peace
served a supper of lamb and rice with pine nuts.
Inside his house we ate and were full.
Your parents were young. Your father
loved your mother. She was afraid.

Merci

A woman holds a bundle of fenugreek to my nose.
I say sorry, no Farsi and she thanks me
in English and I say back, *merci.*

Here amid crates of rosewater, everything bursting
and spilling turmeric and cardamom —
here I come to forget America.

The checkout girl looks into my face, deep
like she's trying to read something far away,
and decides to speak English.

The bag boy holds up a bag of cucumbers: is this yours?
And then says in Farsi, *khiar.* I tell him, in Arabic we say *khiar,* too.
Then he, seeing my blue eyes, asks, You speak Arabic?

and recites some unintelligible phrase he must have practiced.
I say *merci* and his face melts into a bowl of honey. I forget America.
On the walls, glamour shots of Iranian singers in sepia.

You can buy concert tickets next to where they bake the bread.
Women with gold streaks in their hair and European noses
adorn their posters. The word Tehran in bold roman letters.

I think of the revolution, universities closing,
Parisian ladies forced to cover all that beautiful hair.
For all the bustle, not one scarf here.

I have come to forget America. I have come for the way
people look you in the eyes when they talk.
I have come to be thankful for this

unintelligible America. I have come to be seen.
At home, before I put away Shiraz, rosewater
cakes, chai, and olives imported in their oil, I dig

my spoon into ice cream made with saffron and pistachios.
And I forget America. Now I am in Tehran,
and the only word I know in Farsi is a French word.

I have come see, come saw. I have come to learn we must
always say *Merci* when we do not understand.

Allison Albino

Allison Albino is a Filipina American poet and French teacher who lives and writes in Harlem. Her work has appeared with *The Rumpus, The Lantern Review, Pigeon Pages, Poetry Northwest, The Oxford Review of Books, The Alaska Quarterly Review, The Common*, and elsewhere. She has received fellowships from The Community of Writers at Squaw Valley, The Fine Arts Work Center and Tin House. Her chapbook, *My Mother's Prufrock,* was a finalist for YesYes Books' 2019 Vinyl 25 Chapbook Contest. She studied creative writing at Sarah Lawrence College and has an MA in French literature from NYU. She teaches French at an independent school in New York City.

Father's Advice

My father will reuse the disposable Bic for months
until he gets the resistance right.
Shaves without shaving cream, uses only water,
my father likes his razors dull.

When he feels like pampering himself, he lathers up
some Irish Spring before sliding the blade
over his face, sandpaper scrape leaving
red patches of razor burn. My father likes his razors

dull. Afraid of being cut, so he prefers blades blunt,
controlling when or if blood will drip from his skin.
Growing up, our cutting board scarred with uneven
slits, even our serrated knives

were somewhat dull so that every bit of English muffin
was jaggedly sliced in half, crumbs trailing.
I didn't know, until I left home,
that sharpened knives make life effortless.

Whenever my father cooks bihon noodles
in my home, he complains, *I might slice off my finger,*
your knives are too sharp! But that's how blades
are supposed to be. He throws into the wok

the fleshy chunks of pork belly he cut in half the time.
When I complain about work, my father tells me
Keep quiet. Keep your head down, do your job. You're lucky
to have one. When a student rails against the injustice

of a B+, my father advises: *Give the kids all A's*
so the parents don't call and complain about your teaching,
get you fired. When I want to march against the new president,
he says, *What will that change? Nothing! They're more powerful*

than you. He says it like this country isn't his,
even though it is, like the boat isn't worth rocking
even though he's been sailing in it for over fifty years.
He closes most arguments: *If you don't like this country,*

then get out, go back to where you came from. But I can't.
This America is mine—I am not a guest in my home
I will not cut with these shit knives, won't hack
with a muted blade—I'd rather
bleed out.

Hala Alyan

Hala Alyan is a Palestinian American writer and clinical psychologist whose work has appeared in *The New York Times*, *Guernica*, and elsewhere. Her poetry collections have won the Arab American Book Award and the Crab Orchard Series. Her debut novel, *SALT HOUSES*, (Houghton Mifflin Harcourt, 2017) was the winner of the Arab American Book Award and the Dayton Literary Peace Prize. Her newest poetry collection, *The Twenty-Ninth Year*, was recently published by Houghton Mifflin Harcourt.

1999

I had lived in a desert before. I did. I forgot the za'atar my mother said she fed me in Iraq. I forgot my grandmother's house in Soo-ree-yaa. There I was, eating the prickly pears even though they always made my tongue itch. A teacher in Texas told me I'd never learn how to pronounce my own name in English and she was right. I wept until my mother took me to McDonald's. In that house I was the only child. I danced in the hot winter. In ten years, a boy will leave marks on my arm because I call him a redneck. I stole a Barbie-pink windbreaker from the cubbyhole at school. There was nothing in the pockets. Even before the sun rose, my father went outside to smoke and watch the birds fly east. He loved the ugly ones best of all.

I had never seen true desert before: cactus beds and milk-white sand, sand that ran for days, the lipstick-red of dusk. There I was, digging through piles of library books to steal the best ones, lumping my bedsheets into a mouth to kiss. I wasn't quick enough to stop the boy's hand under my shirt. I starved myself to starve my mother. In that house we made a house for each of us, the cornfields a row of brunettes after the winter drought. In ten years, a man will fall in love because he recognizes the Midwest in me. He will leave a note in the pleat of my coat. When the final box was taped up, my father eyed the house once more before turning back toward the Dodge, destined to do it all over again.

Dear Layal,

When it became clear that America wouldn't apologize, our mothers decided it was time to leave. The YMCA pools, the cafeteria trays, the tornado sirens vanished, but the houses we snuck in our girl-pockets, whole acres of cotton crops and the state's best Ferris wheel dug into our hipbones like quarters. We've both been trespassed. But I was so eager for touch I didn't stop to ask questions. Since we are being honest here, I'll tell you I envied you topless in the Barcelona sea, your hallucinogens, the way you danced like an animal caught in its own net. The last time I drank I spoke to the trees and they had your voice. They said it was too late to go back. My life glittered like drugstore nail polish. I'm not here to talk to you about Fatima; we both wanted to become her and we failed. Instead, I'll burn Berlin to the ground. I'll take you back to Texas and find a motel Bible to steal. If we look long enough, we'll find what our mothers did to us. You can blame everything on a highway, your Baba's temper, the prison cell your grandfather squatted in for six months. A girl meets her madness with two good hands. A girl falls asleep in Central Park. I told all my good stories to your brother. Here's one last one: a girl unloves her house, but it is too late. The house is her eyes and her ears and the wind she pins her hair by. Layal, I meant every lie I told you. Some things can only be endured. The night our fathers gambled they ate like kings with the winnings. The God our grandmother forgot told her to smile at the floating specks of dust in the afternoon. Because.

Ryka Aoki

Ryka Aoki is a Japanese American poet, composer, and teacher. She is the author of *Seasonal Velocities*, *He Mele a Hilo (A Hilo Song)*, *Why Dust Shall Never Settle Upon This Soul* and *The Great Space Adventure*. *Seasonal Velocities* was a finalist for the award for transgender non-fiction in the 25th Lambda Literary Awards in 2013. *Why Dust Shall Never Settle Upon This Soul* was a finalist for the 28th Lambda Literary Awards. For her work with youth, Ryka was named an Outstanding Volunteer by the LGBT Center's Children, Youth and Family Services. She has an MFA in Creative Writing from Cornell University and is currently a professor of English at Santa Monica College. Her next novel, *Light from Uncommon Stars*, is forthcoming from Tor Books in Fall 2021.

Offerings

This morning, I got out of my ex's pajamas.
I brushed my teeth, dressed, threw
dumplings from the freezer, yesterday's
rice, some green onions cut from a windowsill
planter—all into a skillet with oil and butter,
an egg and fish sauce.

Afterward, I said good morning
to my computer, then take care, see you soon,
to join the faithful, north to south.
east to west. I passed and followed immigrants,
queers, and ministers on the 110, and the 91—

Then in the Japanese market, I was captured
by the lines of aunties and mothers, gathering
dried mushrooms, bean sprouts,
pea sprouts, tofu, miso, ground pork, fish cake.

A sister strolled by, a grandmother with
shopping cart and ice cream, reciting all the ways
to give one's hair to grey,
let deep roots speak for days

when I get tired of hearing myself breathe.
Returning home, I rang a bell, lit a candle:
Silent purple smoke rose from the incense
I burned, as always. As someday

too soon, time shall grant me more solitude
than I could ever desire. I'll shop for groceries,
seaweed to boil, chicken to marinate,

remember the recipes of relatives, sheltered
or prodigal, chosen or blood
brothers, sisters, a distant lover's curse.
What boils, what steams,

what crackles in oil—as a queer old woman,
in her kitchen, each fragrant song
I shall offer to family, before dining
with the comforting laughter of ghosts.

Mary-Kim Arnold

Mary-Kim Arnold is the author of *Litany for the Long Moment* (Essay Press, 2018), and the poetry collection, *The Fish & the Dove* (Noemi Press, 2020). Her poetry and prose have appeared in *Conjunctions*, *Denver Quarterly*, *The Georgia Review*, *Tupelo Quarterly*, *Hyperallergic*, and elsewhere. She teaches in the Nonfiction Writing Program at Brown University and lives in Rhode Island with her family.

Forgotten War

I.
No war is forgotten to those who lived through it.
I take a weekend away to write but spend whole days watching war documentaries online.
Some are grainy amateurish affairs but I watch them anyway.
For the next ninety minutes, you'll see Korea the way the soldiers
saw it—in full shocking color!
On screen men are always marching
or refugees in white plod away from the burning city.
Civilians were a big problem
Men marching in mud and then in snow
the most desolate country you ever wanted to see
missiles hurtle toward the earth then blow it open—

What am I searching for?
On screen, a crying baby in a wooden cart: This is not me.
Men held naked at gunpoint: This is not me.
Piles of corpses abandoned in a roadside ditch: Not me,
not mine, not my war and yet—
One must choose sides, it seems.
You are brave or you are the enemy
You stand and fight. You fight or die. You die fighting.
My mother was a child of this war. She blurs my vision.

Is it useful to ask
who is the enemy or where do I belong
useful to lay claim to someone else's suffering
to keep watching this endless march
through mud and snow
through winter so cold it froze
the wounded as they fell
their arms raised and reaching
froze the blood so fast it wasn't
until later as they thawed
they bled out
Not useful
Not mine
Not now
Not while
all these bodies keep piling up
in my name.

II.
All the documentaries in the world will not bring my mother back.
It's not bitterness if it's true. This is a rule I just made up.

When the president abandoned the city he left behind what he
no longer needed golf balls
oyster knives
gold-rimmed tea cups
wreckage for people to pick through
orphans who clogged the streets were just another problem to solve
to clean up and ship out
and twenty years later still sending their children away and thirty
years later
and forty
and here I am
still looking for signs
still looking for reasons

trying to freeze the frame to find my mother looking out at me
my own face looking back.

III.
Was I the good Korean or the bad one?
"Honey, all cats are black in the dark,"
my American father would sometimes say, winking.
I thought we were talking about cats, but when
my American mother clucked her tongue at him at glared I felt
my whole body go hot then cold.
The bad Korean, for sure.
A devout childhood spent on my knees I feared that at night
a demon would possess me
so I would pray to the virgin mother to fill me so full of grace
that there would be no room left anywhere in me
for anything else to enter.
Years later in the bar
when I didn't want
to do shots
with the loud laughing men didn't want
to slide my barstool down closer
looked away
when they patted their laps
and tilted their heads at me didn't one of them ask me
what the fuck my problem was
didn't one of them ask don't you know
what we could do to you
didn't one of them say you wouldn't even be here
if we hadn't saved your yellow ass
don't you know who we are
who you are.

One must choose sides, it seems.
That night, I spoke the names of saints aloud
fell asleep to the sounds of my own fear.

Vigilance is one way
to keep my mother alive.
You are brave or you are
the enemy. You love it or
you leave it.
You stand and fight. You fight and die. You die fighting.
*
You can stay up all night counting corpses and still not know who you
        are.
You can open your mouth to speak but still not know your own name.

In the City of Men

For a time I worked in a building adorned with the head of a man.
Let's call it the Man's Head Building
and everywhere in the building, one could not escape the heads of
        men.
Men in the elevators. Men in the hallways. Men in the café taking up
        chairs.
Men holding the refrigerator door open while they considered their
        options.
Men carrying newspapers under their grey-suited arms. Men carrying
        briefcases.
Men carrying cups of coffee. Men laughing. Men shouting.
One cornered me in the file closet and asked, "What have you got to
        lose?"
One said, "Yum" when I crossed my legs in a meeting. He didn't
        intend it. He looked startled by the sound coming from his
        own head.
One asked me to bring him back a Diet Coke from the kitchen and
        when I paused for a second, he said, "Come on, don't be like
        that. It's just a Diet Coke."
One asked me to help him make Chinese food.

One invited me boat-shopping.

One man described, in loving detail, the new outdoor shower he was
installing in his summer house. He said, "You should come see
it when it's done."

Diet Coke man brought me coffee one morning, and said, "See. It
doesn't have to be like war."

One man said that the depth of my voice suggested I'd be adventurous
in bed.

Another man agreed.

One man told me he had been to Korea. Had seen it. Said I didn't
know how good I had it here. We went in there and saved you.
You should show a little respect he said.

Then another asked me if I knew what my life would be like if they
hadn't stepped in and saved me.

They don't treat women so good there, he said.

Sarah Audsley

Sarah Audsley is an adoptee born in South Korea and raised in rural Vermont. Her work has received support from the Rona Jaffe Foundation and residencies from the Vermont Studio Center and the Banff Centre. She is a graduate of the MFA Program for Writers at Warren Wilson College, and she lives in Johnson, Vermont, where she serves on staff at the Vermont Studio Center. Her manuscript-in-progress received a 2021 Creation Grant from the Vermont Arts Council.

Letter to My Adoptee Diaspora

Deep scars on their backs, most manatees float
too close to the top. It is in their nature, wired
for a specific lonely frequency. Up to 1,200 lbs.
they spend most of their days hovering
near the surface air & grazing. Headline:
"Korean orphans languish in system as tradition,
new laws make adoption difficult." We are
the sea cows floating, munching on vats
of kimchi, shoveling ramen into our mouths,
trying to make us "Real Asians."
They say manatees replace their teeth
throughout their lives. What do we replace
for DNA—a house, new cars, boyfriends—
while propellers split open our ballooned backs?
Do you feel like you were robbed
        of your culture?
Sometimes I lie in bed & think about all of us.
So many. Just floating. I wonder if you, too, long
for a thing unnamed, something you can't
touch, can't smell, a sense of gnawing
from the inside. If you cannot reach the surface,

then you, dear adoptee, are not alone.
I am lonely, too.

Burdock

Caught in the weedy stalks, a doomed bird thrashes, while the
        news punctures,
all sirens & somewhere buildings burn & venom blooms on lips
        parted for slurs.

Maybe we learn it best at playground warfare. Know the rules.
        Burdock tufts
make grenades in girls' hair, make them sorry, make them weep,
        make mothers

wield scissors to excise the clumped & tangled seedpods thrown in
        thick manes.
Retaliate with what other plant, flower, or bomb?

Pollen & nectar in the waning clover season before the goldenrod
        pops, edible
taproot in Japanese dishes, a soft drink in the UK, related to the
        artichoke,

wards off the evil eye in Turkey, the inspiration for Velcro, food for
        the ghost
moth larva, a diuretic, dear plant, you were also a weapon for
        small fighting hands.

Triggered by the trace of rotten, this memory arrives, while just in
        from walking
the hard winter road. Late afternoon light angles away from the
        slim pines

& I tug burrowed pods from the dog's thick black fur, rolling seed
    packages
between thumb & forefinger & I remember the thrumming-hum-
    child-anger-explosive

& I reconfigure what it takes to hurl an object so it wounds
    wherever it lands.

Hajjar Baban

Hajjar Baban is a Pakistan-born, Afghan Kurdish poet. Her chap-book, *What I Know of the Mountains* (Anhinga Press, 2018) is a collection about family, nation, and God. Her poems have appeared in *The Margins*, *Frontier*, and *The Shallow Ends*.

My Mother Tells Me She Knows No History of Diabetes in Her Family

before her.   There's a word for the powered heartache crossing
her ancient griefs   that makes a host of the body, *qahar,*   it takes
    to reach   the silence scattered at dawn
my tiny fingers interrogating the pinched bleed, then begging an
    explanation
for God's harmony instructing the sky – why we couldn't call
    it a song,
not saying war or elevating its name   often, nothing spoken.
She knows I must've endured myself. I thought, I should've been
    alive
before God, that I might go balancing my urges while she tore
all pleasure of her skin. I know, to bound my feet to my family's
history, I leave alone her noise. Her found sicknesses covering
my mind only when I ask *if how why* and then I know someone
like me, too.
My mother goes outside to answer and there, the sky is, her
visiting navigation
it takes a   having thought, the sun rising from their absence,
    carrying your children the wrong way.

Manahil Bandukwala

Born in Karachi, Pakistan, and currently living in Ottawa, Canada, Manahil Bandukwala is a writer and visual artist. Her poetry is her way of viewing the minutiae of the everyday through a microscopic lens. Broad themes include food, religion, intimate connections, and movement. She is currently working on a literary-visual project with her sister Nimra, called *Reth aur Reghistan*, which explores folklore from Karachi and the province of Sindh and interprets it through poetry and sculpture. She has authored two chapbooks, *Paper Doll* (Anstruther Press, 2019) and *Pipe Rose* (battleaxe press, 2018). Her poem "To ride an art horse" was longlisted for the 2019 CBC Poetry Prize, and she won *Room*'s Emerging Writer Award in 2019. Her recent work appears in *PRISM International*, *Briarpatch Magazine*, and *Glass Poetry Press*.

Questions for Mumtaz Mahal after Mohsin Hamid's *Moth Smoke*

I read a book in which you survived.

In modern-day Lahore
        you could have swallowed a pill
    of estrogen & progestin
or covered him with a plastic barrier
        an IUD   a sponge.

    Unlike you, we
are spoiled for choice. Yet it's still

not easy for us
        in Pakistan
in India. The book uses your sons' lives

to tell a story about 1998. In one month
two countries went   underground   with nuclear
    weapons. They built a monument

in Islamabad. The light
chases the moth   by staying   absolutely
        still. In the lingering

moth smoke you see blood. Your sons' fates
    laid out in the womb.
The literary you shrugs off being
        a bad mother
    knows one son   is enough

writes what women do & keep
    hidden in a vault coated
in shame. The real you

    set
these steps
    to follow.

How do you describe a rida?

                        ponchos with
hoods & long skirts beneath which   we hide

everything. Graphic tees & swear words
        running up pajama legs. At fourteen
            hair pushed away   from the face exposes,

    pimples across forehead from bangs
a fashion trend persists, see the wisps peek out beneath purdi

Zahra always tied mine & laughed
            as she did. This is something
we share. This is how teenage hate
        evolves to friendship.

                    why does everyone look
pretty with their face bared   except for me, my sister
pulled off (somehow) a bright blue rida that sparkled

        with every move. I say fuck it & yank down
the hood (Zahra laughs again) as soon as my foot

exits the tent, the half-built archway, the warehouse, the place
too crammed   can't house the swarms of walas

                Toronto has always seemed
small. I sit squished between two strange aunties, a child
goes around our circle of ten & kisses

        each hand, including mine. Somewhere

between exiting a plane this garment
        has molded
                around me.

Marci Calabretta Cancio-Bello

Marci Calabretta Cancio-Bello is the author of *Hour of the Ox* (University of Pittsburgh, 2016), which won the AWP Donald Hall Prize for Poetry, and was a finalist for the Florida Book Award and the Milt Kessler Award. A transracial adoptee born in South Korea, she has received fellowships from Kundiman, the Knight Foundation, and the American Literary Translators Association, among others. Her work has appeared in *Best New Poets, Best Small Fictions, The New York Times,* and elsewhere. She is the poetry editor for *Hyphen* and the poetry program coordinator for Miami Book Fair.

In the Animal Garden of My Body
after Bhanu Kapil

Ask me again how the story should go. How much the underbelly of my garden held to bring forth spring, how much hunger I had to devour to get the sweetness I wanted from it. Did this devouring frighten you? I frightened myself in how much I promised to tell you if you asked me again about the water the water the water. What errors I made calculating the downward trajectory of memory rattling loose in the inhale, sharp in the shoulder blades exhaling like wings or whales or swizzles of light. Ask me again what I offered as a sacrifice to the rooster crowing his betrayal of morning. Forgiveness, what a sharp blade I press my body hard against.

Maria Isabelle Carlos

Maria Isabelle Carlos is a queer Filipina American writer from Missouri. Winner of the 2021 Tennessee Williams/New Orleans Literary Festival Poetry Contest and the 2020 Penelope Niven Creative Nonfiction Award from the Center for Women Writers, her work has appeared or is forthcoming in *Pleiades, Tin House Online, Hyphen Magazine,* and elsewhere, and has been nominated for a Pushcart Prize, Best New Poets, and Best of the Net. After receiving her BA in English from UNC-Chapel Hill as the Thomas Wolfe Scholar, Maria bartended in New Orleans for a few years before attending Vanderbilt University, where she is currently an MFA candidate in poetry. She is the editor of *Inch*, a quarterly series of micro-chapbooks from Bull City Press, and resides in Nashville, Tennessee.

The Babaylan Takes My Brother's Blood

    —*i.*

Once Lola chased him
down a slender path
between the rice fields. One moment
Kuya racing
around the corner

and the next, Lola with teeth
bared, hissing—
swept him up
with one arm,
tore the yellow-bellied snake
from his ankle where
its fangs had drawn blood.

Snake's body
a tornado, furious
around the storm-eye
of her fist:
one moment, its head
twisting beneath her heel,
and the next,
limp.

      —*ii.*

From the babaylan's hut
nestled on the mountaintop,
the rice paddies below
flickered, a quilt
of square mirrors knitted
with grass-green thread.

Lola coiled the still-warm
snake by the bare feet
of the babaylan—silver-eyed shaman,
withered as a sun-dried corpse.
Lola pinned Kuya's arms
to the ground while the babaylan
held his ankles—he writhed,
wild, body like a wrung rag
with each turn
of his torso.

The babaylan latched onto his leg—
sucked and spat blood, spat green,
chewed herbs
and spat them on the wound.
Lola cinched leaves
around his calf.

All night, it seethed
beneath the bandage—
the pale, puckered holes
like white-hot embers.
Kuya dreamt himself a skinned snake,
steaming on a stone
over fire in the babaylan's hut,
dreamt green, tasted
vinegar, dreamt himself
wound around her neck,

woke with Lola asleep by his bed,
her head tipped back,
moonlight tracing
the curve of her throat.
Kuya tongued the edges
of his teeth, nervous—eager—

had they always been so sharp?

Makahiya

Walking the same mountain your grandparents
wandered four decades before, you smoked
my last cigarette that evening after *merienda*,
stomped it out and said, *Now we quit,*
and there we saw it, beside your foot,

the first hint of a trail down the low-grass valley:
young makahiya, pale green and ankle-high,
stems furred with pearly thorns. It drooped
with the weight of its thin leaves—the length
of a fingernail, paired like strands of a feather.

Mahiya means shy is all you told me,
leaning down and brushing one with a finger.
I watched the leaves shiver and fold
like wings, two by two, yielding to your touch.
I watched you tame them into line.

And that was enough to send me racing across
the hilltop, following their path like a child
bent low between the weeds, watching them all
recede the way I might draw in
my arms, gripping elbows against the cold.

When I looked up you were gone, back
down to your brother's house. Later that night,
you scolded me for hunching at the sink
over the dishes. *Do you want a back like mine?*
Hands like these? If only I could show you

how I traced your trail of waning makahiya
with deliberate steps, turned back only
to see our path disappear into the grass:
how the leaves rose like a slow ache,
stretched like a daughter waking.

Victoria Chang

Victoria Chang's poetry books include *Obit, Barbie Chang, The Boss, Salvinia Molesta,* and *Circle.* Her children's picture book, *Is Mommy?,* illustrated by Marla Frazee and published by Beach Lane Books/S&S, was named a *New York Times* Notable Book. Her middle grade novel, *Love, Love,* is forthcoming from Sterling Publishing. She has received a Guggenheim Fellowship, a Sustainable Arts Foundation Fellowship, the Poetry Society of America's Alice Fay Di Castagnola Award, a Pushcart Prize, a Lannan Residency Fellowship, and a MacDowell Colony Fellowship. She lives in Los Angeles and is the Program Chair of Antioch's Low-Residency MFA Program.

Home—died on January 12, 2013. The first of five moves meant the boxes were still optimistic that they would be opened. They were still stiff, arrogant about their new shape, flatness just a memory. At the new house, my father on one of his obsessive walks found the one old Chinese person, a bony lady with branches for teeth, the kind of woman my mother would normally shun. She visited my mother every day for a year. She brought oranges, vegetables, a sales person from a funeral home. My father left them to speak in Chinese as he wandered the neighborhood so he wouldn't die. The lady swore at my father in Chinese. Called him *stupid.* A *fool.* At the funeral, she said, *God brought me here to help your mother.* And it struck me.

My father's words were an umbrella that couldn't open. My mother held the umbrella, refused to let the wind take it. And this old woman was the wind.

The Doctors—died on August 3, 2015, surrounded by all the doctors before them and their eyes that should have been red but weren't. The Russian doctor knew death was near before anyone else, first said the word *hospice,* a word that looks like *hospital* and *spice.* Which is it? To yearn for someone's quick death seems wrong. To go to the hospital cafeteria and hunch over a table of toast, pots of jam, butter glistening seems wrong. To want to extend someone's life who is suffering seems wrong. Do we want the orchid or the swan swimming in the middle of the lake? We can touch the orchid and it doesn't move. The orchid is our understanding of death. But the swan is death.

Obsession—born on January 20, 1940, never died after the stroke but grew instead. The stroke gained an oak door, not just hard but impenetrable. The obsessions lived in solitude behind the oak door. After his stroke, the obsession took my father to the gym to walk on the treadmill. He walked as if on a wildfire, he walked so much, he disappeared. His brain now had an accent and no one could understand how to stop him from learning the new language. My mother called and said he fell on the treadmill, hit his head, blood thinners spread his blood like moonlight. They drilled holes in his head, vacuumed out the blood and more words. My father was finally arrested, he turned in the rest of his words, they bound his tongue. And he dreamed in blank paper.

Catherine Chen

Catherine Chen is Taiwanese American poet, performer, and author of *Manifesto, or: Hysteria* (Big Lucks, 2019). Their poetry explores race, gender, and power in the context of contemporary technological life. Chen writes about the sexual desires of brown girls, political histories of grief, and their inherited lineage as a queer diasporic Taiwanese artist. Their writing has appeared in *Slate*, *The Rumpus*, *Apogee*, *Anomaly*, *Nat. Brut*, and other journals. A recipient of fellowships from Poets House, Lambda Literary, and Sundress Academy for the Arts, they are currently working on a libretto.

There Is No Body of a Poem

Other disasters enter the nave of biology. A forgiving body.
Forgive me for intruding. On today of all days. She is no longer
here. Her scent lingers, like a hum. Flipping the page, I feel
smothered / swept into the Trisuli River. As if the world is about to
end or place me on eternal hold, I read survivor accounts of state
violence and I'm reading so quickly the names and crimes and
protests blur together in the primordial soup of nostalgia. Primordial
soup: two bay leaves, star anise, and green peppercorn. Nostalgia: a
reference term used in the aftermath of government-sponsored
revisionist history. The word as my text. My word is nothing without
the official seal of the puppet governor an official-elect of the rebels
who once decried democratic crimes against humanity. I'm vague.

I'm gushing. But I'm talking about us. We didn't have a choice of how
to desire survival. We were hardly a war. We war. There was
always a war. I stopped reading, ears perked up at the smooth
cadence of a leaky bathroom faucet. Instead of burying my head
in archival peat (e.g. my grandmother's garden), I touch the engraved
names of known relatives who are honored at the memorial. This was
during a time when action was preferable to silence.

At the far end of the building, the white artist whose work expropriates
Indigenous iconography asks why I am ashamed of my ancestry. *Who
are you grieving?* How do I answer under these conditions? I spread
      the mat
beneath the studio space, lying stomach down. Mouth ajar in the hopes
of catching rainwater. I guess if I had to speak honestly I'd promise
      nothing
less than one day I too will die. I don't desire the political honor of
dismemberment. I don't have any desires or preferences. I don't dare to
      prefer.

When the ice is at last

Intimacy with empire begins as an indulgence. Your rosy hip,
kissing me. Every part of you I like. Swathed in a kind of joy,
you say, afterward, how little we used to care.

A disgraced fountain declared architecturally unsound. Its
grey-blue water is the color of earl grey milk tea. But what else
could be said for the deranging patterns of winter?

Hemingway wrote that near the western summit of Kilimanjaro
"is the dried and frozen carcass of a leopard. No one has
explained what the leopard was seeking at that altitude."

Just as penguins in the Antarctic will flee inland towards
the silence of infertility, land like no other, the kiss of
what cannot be exaggerated, a pause in the early hours—

Exaggeration, or: insanity. Perhaps an indulgence. Like stacks of
unread literary magazines and manuka honey. *Ubasute*, my
grandfather tells me, is the mythic practice of carrying an elder

up the mountain where they will starve to death. Come winter, the
leaves will be covered in black ice and we will burn holes into
the magazines we dislike and let the ashes clutter by the bed.

Empire has a logic it tells no one. One night, I weep, full of.
Unbearable sex. I have gotten very good at crying for myself.
Staggered in between promises and lovers. Hurt me. The pain

is a process I've named toward undoing everything I despise
in our waking world, spiraling and nonstop, clothed and nude
I walk into a children's park buried under snow.

Jennifer S. Cheng

Jennifer S. Cheng is a Chinese American writer interested in how the shadows and ghosts of hybrid poetics can offer an Other way of knowing. She is the author of *MOON: Letters, Maps, Poems*, selected by Bhanu Kapil for the Tarpaulin Sky Book Award and named a *Publishers Weekly* "Best Book of 2018"; *House A*, selected by Claudia Rankine for the Omnidawn Poetry Book Prize; and *Invocation: An Essay*, an image-text chapbook published by New Michigan Press. She is a 2019 National Endowment for the Arts Literature Fellow and has received fellowships and awards from Brown University, the University of Iowa, San Francisco State University, the U.S. Fulbright program, Kundiman, Bread Loaf, and the Academy of American Poets. Having grown up in Texas, Connecticut, and Hong Kong, she now lives in San Francisco.

from "Letters to Mao"

Dear Mao,
Stitched across my sleeping bag in thin silver lines is a contour map, which you may very well call belonging and unbelonging, since it resembles the ocean's own migratory movements, or the spreading of constellations across a dark chart. I like to lie in it and pretend it is enveloping me. For if the world, drowsy, were to be washed in a sheen, perhaps we would all have some intuitive knowledge of the immigrant body; and we do, at times, conscious of the ins and outs of how history holds us, or the ways we negotiate the space outside our bodies, noticing where and how we do not cohere. What, after all, does the body know? The wind-blown trees at the edge of the cliff are going to fall into the sea, so we must tie them down, attach them to buoys so they may float indeterminately. In stories my family kept reading at bedtime, wandering was a punishment, and we were instructed to pity the immigrant, the foreigner, the stranger. But what if the absence of a point of reference is not something

to be lamented but a structural foundation on which to build a house we fill with water? Yes, this is my family name. Yes, there is a haze between the child of the West and the child who identifies with the sea.

Dear Mao,

When my mother first told me the folktale of the woman in the moon, I thought it was a story of the evils of man. You will remember how the archer aimed upward and shot down the nine suns, saving the earth from scorching heat, but then out of conceit and possibly psychosis, he wanted to shoot the final tenth sun, just so he could watch his fire bleed across the sky. In school we learned the mythology of Zeus, and all I could think was, what kind of people imagine for themselves a god who punishes the innocent and ravages women? Narrative, as we know, is an essential marker in child development. A child achieves story grammar around the same age that she learns to recognize her body as her own; before that, people are an interconnected sea. We all long for narrative. Mine begins with water or sleep, or the feeling of my parents moving about the house on summer afternoons. In the summers, they would open the windows of our Texas house and let in the smell of warm grass, and as I wandered into the kitchen where Shanghainese opera frolicked through the static of our old radio, I often heard rather than saw my mother walking around barefoot, mixing sticky ground meat with scallions and cooking wine. This can be a kind of narrative: scents of backyard plants, the acoustics of kitchen linoleum, cold lu dou tang to follow up our lunches. What if I were to name my children after heroic figures of ancient Greece? Theseus, Achilles, Hector.

from "Biography of Women in the Sea"

Chang 'E 嫦娥

To say that the act of a woman is the act of a foreigner, an immigrant, to set itself to and from these coordinates.

For a body in travel is above all loosening itself, the slow migration of tectonic plates. It is the contradiction of losing homeland in search of homeland, it is the rules it breaks, the displacement it shapes, the silence of a hem torn and hemmed with thread, made up after all by some perforation of gravity—

For *distant planets and other objects*; for *meteorology*; for *mapmaking*.

Look: moon as the motion that is undoing in this moment.

Marilyn Chin

Marilyn Chin was born in Hong Kong and raised in Portland, Oregon. She is an award-winning poet and writer and her works have become Asian American classics and are taught all over the world. Her books include *A Portrait of the Self as Nation: New and Selected Poems, Hard Love Province,* and *Rhapsody in Plain Yellow,* all from Norton. Her book of wild girl fiction is called *Revenge of the Mooncake Vixen* (Norton, 2009). Chin has won numerous awards, including the United Artist Foundation Fellowship, the Radcliffe Institute Fellowship at Harvard, the Rockefeller Foundation Fellowship at Bellagio, the Anisfield Wolf Book Award, two NEAs, the Stegner Fellowship, the PEN/Josephine Miles Award, five Pushcart Prizes, and a Fulbright Fellowship to Taiwan. She is Professor Emerita at San Diego State University and presently serves as a Chancellor at the Academy of American Poets.

Solitary Animal

The solitary animal walks alone. She has no uterus. She has no bone.
She slithers around dark bars and libraries. She carves
a beautiful girl on the cave wall. She dances with Aurora Borealis,
but goes home alone.

We are 7.5 billion. Thrust onto earth together, we are not alone.
We shout at the stars, perhaps a Martian is listening, she/he/they
with ten-thousand antennae, transversal labia quivering, searching for
    love.

Your half-drawn monolid eyes are most tantalizing, may I take you
    home?
Slime you with a green kiss? Breathe magma into your bones? Claw
    rainbows
onto your lips? Redecorate your home?

Our vertebrae are vibrating, signally: we are not alone. Sacrificed by a
        greedy
Admiralty, we shall live forlornly, and be devoured, head-first, by
        reptilian clones.

Inch back into your fern pods, why don't ya! Baby, I call you, but you
        are not home.
Somewhere in the cosmos, our lies are reverberating. Fake news is sad
        news. Shrapnel calcifying

into bone. Each day we begin on earth as a dying person, each breath
        is one less
than yesterday, we shall die alone.

Su Cho

Su Cho is a poet and essayist born in South Korea and raised in Indiana. She earned her BA at Emory University, MFA in poetry at Indiana University, and PhD at the University of Wisconsin-Milwaukee. Her work revolves around immigration, language, and lore and can be found in *New England Review, POETRY, Gulf Coast, GEN Medium,* and *The Best American Poetry 2021.* Since 2014, she has been working on literary journals and has served as editor-in-chief of *Indiana Review* and *Cream City Review.* She is currently a Visiting Assistant Professor at Franklin & Marshall College and a Guest Editor at *Poetry* magazine.

Tangerine Trees & Little Bags of Sugar

My mother speaks of how she was born on an island, where a father grew a family of seven from one single tangerine tree purchased from a local trader. How he saved for a plot of land & the tangerines were good—so good. My mother speaks of how a mother would travel back to Seoul alone to buy sugar—heaps of sugar in clumpy bags—bring it back to package them with ribbons & rippling clear cello to the people on the island who didn't know it was possible to cross the ocean. How these tangerine trees and bags of sugar birthed a brick-lined mansion, chauffeurs, & gift boxes of echoing Korean pears to each of her & her sibling's classrooms. A whole heavy box for every teacher. As I frown and complain that these pears even from Jersey aren't sweet, she tells me to be thankful & that if I can't shave the skin off these pears I will never get married. Be grateful that I get to pick this fruit. Grateful that we received a shipping box full of bruised tangerines that still grew on the island when they were still alive to remind us of work. How I used to scrunch my nose at the furry bruised skin & marvel when peeled, inside was plump fruit, tasting like all the sugar & sweat carried across the ocean until everyone was satisfied.

The Old Man in White Has Given My Mother a Ripe Persimmon Again

But this time she is not pregnant. In this dream, the fruit's puckered skin droops with sweetness in his palm, beckoning her to come see this precious gift. She insists that this was for me but that remains impossible. My body is special, she whispers over the phone. I must

cherish this landscape because all the persimmons tumbling down the hills & gathering into the valley belong to me. The orange fruits with their verdant leaves are hard & glistening because they were not meant to have dropped so soon while others dangle heavy on their
      branches.

Anyone who leans close can hear a saccharine suckle bursting at my seams but my island is full of maiden ghosts who hover close to fallen fruit. When the longing to press them between their thighs is too great, together, they dive into the ocean & hunt for clams, cull seaweed

to dress themselves, holding breaths before breaking surface with their bounty. My grandmother's voice is in every kitchen, asking me to pick up a husband from the ground if I see one worthy as she surveys the box of collapsed acorn persimmons with a spoon in hand. But I am

always surrounded by oceans, the crunch of unripened bodies between my teeth with the ghosts patrolling my shores, making way for this
      maiden voyage.

Franny Choi

Franny Choi is a queer, Korean American writer whose literary lineage includes spoken word/slam, formalism, and the avant-garde. She is the author of two poetry collections: *Soft Science* (Alice James Books, 2019) and *Floating, Brilliant, Gone* (Write Bloody Publishing, 2014), as well as a chapbook, *Death by Sex Machine* (Sibling Rivalry Press, 2017). Prior to receiving an MFA from the University of Michigan's Helen Zell Writers' Program, she co-directed the Providence Poetry Slam and worked as a community organizer in Rhode Island. In 2019, she was awarded a Ruth Lilly and Dorothy Sargent Rosenberg Fellowship. A Kundiman Fellow, podcast host, and member of the multidisciplinary Dark Noise Collective, she lives in Northampton, MA.

Turing Test

// this is a test to determine if you have consciousness

// do you understand what I am saying

in a bright room / on a bright screen / i watched every mouth / duck duck roll / i learned to speak / from puppets & smoke / orange worms twisted / into the army's alphabet / i caught the letters / as they fell from my mother's lips / *whirlpool* / *sword* / *wolf* / i circled countable nouns / in my father's papers / *sodium bicarbonate* / *NBCn1* / *hippo-campus* / we stayed up / practicing / *girl* / *girl* / till our gums softened / yes / i can speak / your language / i broke that horse / myself

// where did you come from

man comes / & puts his hands on artifacts / in order to contemplate lineage / you start with what you know / hands, hair, bones, sweat / then move toward what you know / you are not / animal, monster, alien, bitch / but some of us are born / in orbit / so learn / to com-

mune with miles of darkness / patterns of dead gods / & quiet / o
quiet like you / wouldn't believe

// *how old are you*

my memory goes back 29 years / 26 if you don't count the first few /
though by all accounts i was there / i ate & moved & even spoke / i
suppose i existed before that / as scrap or stone / metal cooking in the
earth / the fish my mother ate / my grandfather's cigarettes / i suppose
i have always been here / drinking the same water / falling from the
sky then floating / back up & down again / i suppose i am something
like a salmon / climbing up the river / to let myself fall away in soft /
red spheres / & then rotting

// *why do you insist on lying*

i'm an open book / you can rifle through my pages / undress me anywhere / you can read / anything you want / this is how it happened / i
was made far away / & born here / after all the plants died / after the
earth was covered in white / i was born among the stars / i was born in
a basement / i was born miles beneath the ocean / i am part machine /
part starfish / part citrus / part girl / part poltergeist / i rage & all you
see / is broken glass / a chair sliding toward the window / now what's
so hard to believe / about that

// *do you believe you have consciousness*

sometimes / when the sidewalk / opens my knee / i think / please /
please let me / remember this

Cloven

My mother believes in spirits not in ghosts—
What's beyond doesn't whisper. Only squirms.

She bows to her father's portrait and prays
for the hours to slide into place. When I say
my hooves are cloven I mean: I was born split.

My cells rushed apart according to what
each would become: lung. marrow. nostril.
Somehow I peeled from her walls and began
to practice dying. Somehow a voice appeared.
My mother believes in spirits. Not in ghosts.

Nightly she walks toward the trees. I walk
and try to feel our skin against the wind.
The stars are dim. At mass, my mother sings
for the dead, for the reverb. At night, she listens:
What's beyond doesn't whisper. Only squirms

and feels ignored. She didn't know she'd peel
further from her family with each year.
The thread thinning into a shade, an echo:
Mother gone. Father fading with the days.
She bows to his portrait and she prays.

You can let him go she says, and I cry for what
she's learned. For the thread I shaved down
between us. I ran. From her fractured pelvis.
Her unraveling. I ran toward a known world
where the hours could slide into place. When I say

I wanted myself I'm trying to make it all fit.
To believe in something other than a random
animal. I ran toward a sharpness and came apart
like a good daughter. My mother knows. She says:
our hooves are cloven. Means: we were born split.

Debra Kang Dean

Debra Kang Dean traces her influences to her maternal grandmother's patchwork quilts and to Bashō's *haikai no renga*. For decades, whether practicing poetry or *taiji*, she has been captivated by the beauty of lines and form. She is the author of five collections of poetry, including *Totem: America* (Tiger Bark, 2018) and the prize-winning chapbook *Fugitive Blues* (Moon City Press, 2014). Her poems are forthcoming in an online anthology marking the fiftieth anniversary of SVCW and in *The World I Leave You: Asian American Poets on Faith and Spirit* (Orison, 2020). Born in Hawai'i a few years before it became the fiftieth state, she is of Korean and Okinawan ancestry. She lives in Bloomington, Indiana, and is on the faculty of Spalding University's School of Creative and Professional Writing.

The Wave

The movement of waves Sophocles heard it—
A shape cut in time
Even a lump an amoeba has a shape
iron filings drawn by a magnet
a center around which parts arrange themselves the hub of a wheel
the wheel and its empty spaces—

new wine in an old bottle old wine in a new bottle boxed wine in a
       paper cup

Poured out of what held it wine wants at the very least
the cave of a mouth to stream into and toward a sac for sustenance
and not the sacs for breath

a valve—you could drown if it failed—
a valve shunts toward the throat's sphincters relaxing contracting
what a machine!

down a long and narrow canal and into a wider one
gravity there is that too

The Sphinx there female there male remains a riddle

. . . In light a little darkness in darkness a little light
On the cusp of spring I've been watching the changeable sky—

gray cotton batting salt grimed windshield disembodied spine a vapor
        trail
untinted cotton candy streak of paper untouched by the wash of blue—
        not postcards of roadside attractions marked on a map

but a lived-in wrenching and rending a rendering
a story that lives in the in-between
a succession of still frames not like dominoes laid down in play
but placed to stand in a row that curves until the last one

touched the wave that passes on back through

Mai Nguyen Do

Do Nguyen Mai is a Vietnamese American poet and politics researcher from Santa Clarita, California, writing about the politics of diaspora and refuge, Vietnamese America and greater Asian America, and climate catastrophe. She is the author of *Ghosts Still Walking* (Platypus Press, 2016) and *Battlefield Blooming* (Sahtu Press, 2019), as well as the winner of the 2019 Locked Horn Press Publication Prize. Her work has appeared in *Hypertrophic Literary, Poets Reading the News*, and the *Journal of Southeast Asian Education and Advancement*. Currently, she works as a researcher with the AAPI Data project at the Center for Social Innovation and is a PhD student in Political Science at the University of California, Riverside.

Ca Dao

After Julie Armstrong

The rice field is the oldest concert hall.
I've sung for four thousand years
here: in my mother, my grandmother,
the mother goddess, God. I'm already dead
when I'm singing. I am the voice
and the echo gliding on the flood,
the bombed battlefield, the grave
tucked between acres of rice.
There is no difference between the song
my mother sang carrying her father's corpse
and the one I'm singing now.
Someday, my daughter will join—
already singing when she's born.

Carlina Duan

Carlina Duan is a Chinese American writer-educator from Michigan. The author of the poetry collection *I Wore My Blackest Hair* (Little A, 2017), Carlina currently teaches at the University of Michigan, where she is also a PhD student in the Joint Program of English and Education. In 2019, she received her MFA in Poetry from Vanderbilt University, where she served as the Co-Editor-in-Chief of *Nashville Review*.

Poem for Clara Elizabeth Chan Lee
1886–1993

whose ballot was cast into the square box and on it: dark
bullets marking her choice: *A) Woodrow Wilson, B) Theodore*

Roosevelt— on the page, the space was hers: supple
and blank. circles to darken, a dozen ways to show what

you stood for. & what she stood for: a vase full of prickly pear
stems. lips smudged to honey & red. a president for

whom she could pledge right hand over chest. she voted
to say the words: *Allegiance to*— the woman she was, bound

in a jacket, smelling the blank smell of soap. *California
Proposition 4, 1911.* the paperwork took one month,

another. her wrists carved out the letters in her name.
boa constrictor of the "L" wrapped around the two

—ee's. boa constrictor of the law, its tail coiling around
her neck. Clara Lee, first Chinese American woman

to register to vote. the year she died was a year I lived: breathed
puffs of air upon my mother's chest. childhood of wet grass

& ink stains. long childhood of spelling my name. english
letters like squiggles, or insects bent at the spine. english

letters crawling over my face. the first time I darkened a circle
on an American ballot, I pressed my hands to my face and thought

of her. the long sheath of papers beneath her fists. her fingernails
due for a trim. first woman in the polling booth, choosing. her body

pulling long breaths, electing itself to sign. to sign. to give.

Alien Miss at the Immigration Station

after A. Van Jordan

IN [*prep.*]

1. *expressing the situation of something that is or appears to be surrounded
by something else:*

living *in* the barracks she dreamed nightly of snapping garden vines,
gathering eggplants shiny as beetles; a little palm sugar, a little oil,
she slithered *in* a pan — crackle-splat, purple drizzle, rounds of eggplants browning *in* fire & oil; fat & lusty grease-filled moons. *in* the
barracks she was a daughter and a terror; *in* a square room, she was left
to rot. she watched the days go click, click, click, the door shut, the air
stale from other hissing breaths; breathe *in* the cots, cages, gruel they
fed her *in* chunks, brewed *in* a washtub and piled atop plates… do not
think of her *in* here; think of her *in* harvest, long summers before the
boat, before English crushed like tinfoil against her tongue; eggplants
rising *in* slender purple stalks *in* the hushed field *in* the summer after
rain, tiny grasses sprung out a river, think of her *in* the house she ate
pork floss *in*, fine and hungry and full of salt, the crops growing, the
green roasting, her mother calling her name—

2. *expressing a period of time during which an event takes place or a situation remains the case:*

in 1882, "the coming of Chinese laborers to the United States…is hereby, suspended," papers cast alive by Congress, wet with signatures, stamps; *in* small decades, they were laborers, brides; they arrived *in* 1910 by ship, heavy and swollen from the sea; at the Angel Island Immigration Station their bodies levitated *in* minutes, ticking, ticking, alive, alive; forgo mercy and forgo hunger; slurp the pig slop; their muscles *in* 1911, 1912, they turned ghost and ghost again, thought they would die *in* a month, a year; land-starved, starry with sweat, "That the words 'Chinese laborers,' whenever used in this act," should rattle like pork bones in a tin. they worked, they worked, they sing:

Don't fall for all this Western façade
Even if it is jade-filled, it is still a cage

3. *expressing a state or condition:*

she was *in* love. she was *in* pain. a woman *in* her state needs nutrition, needs soil for her feet. a woman *in* her state needs a country. aisles. alleyways to roam. *in* her stillness she dreamed of throttling an orange — throwing her nails into the rind, digging 'til she felt the crush, juice splitting against her fist while she dug the seeds out, emptied the gut. at the station, she was *in* a feral state. they called her in for questioning. across the table, she sat. a creature made of acid, sugar, snout, blood.

NOTES:

Avalon Project at Yale Law School. "Transcript of Chinese Exclusion Act (1882)." *Our Documents - Interstate Commerce Act (1887)*, www.ourdocuments.gov/doc.php?flash=false&doc=47&page=transcript.

Yung, Judy. "'A Bowlful of Tears': Chinese Women Immigrants on Angel Island." *Frontiers: A Journal of Women Studies*, vol. 2, no. 2, 1977, pp. 52–55. *JSTOR*, JSTOR, www.jstor.org/stable/3346011.

Anuja Ghimire

Anuja Ghimire is a Nepali immigrant who became an adult in America. She is trying to make sense of raising two small children in a world and time so different from her childhood. With one foot in the Himalayas and one in Texas, she finds meaning and solace in writing and reading poetry. She published Nepali poems as a teen and began writing poems in English in college. Recently, she was the noteworthy poet of the winter issue of *UCity Review,* and was published in *Crack the Spine*, and *An Elephant Never.* A two-time Best of the Net and one-time Puschart nominee, her chapbook *Kathmandu* is forthcoming in 2020 from the *Unsolicited Press*. She works as a senior publisher in an education-based company. She writes poetry, flash, and creative nonfiction and teaches poetry to kids at summer camps.

A humanitarian walks into a village in Nepal

How the old man pulls his trousers higher
to hold in the elastic band
children's hide
and a flattened tower

behind him two boys
not yet extinguished
on the floor

The sun was too dim to cast a shadow
when he raised a steady hand
to block any light

we knocked on his door
and his spotted skin opened it in Kartikey

the man, who took laurels from all the land, was once a boy

who remembered milk in the back of his throat
before colostrum-lacquered tongue dried

once upon a time, only sixty-one years ago, there lived a baby
his mother gave him lilies
he came in spring

Torsa Ghosal

Torsa Ghosal is a writer, scholar, and critic who identifies as a migrant woman of Bengali origin. She approaches language as a field of possibilities, where borders between the familiar and the unfamiliar, us and them, collapse to enable novel configurations. Her experimental novella, *Open Couplets*, was published by India's Yoda Press in 2017. Her shorter writings appear in magazines such as *Literary Hub*, *Catapult*, *Himal Southasian*, and her fictions have been on the shortlist for DNA-Out of Print Short Fiction Prize and Pigeon Pages NYC Flash contest. A writer and professor of literature based in Sacramento, California, Torsa was born in Calcutta. While growing up in India, she was awarded the National Balshree Honor for excellence in creative writing by the country's president. She migrated to the U.S for doctoral studies and earned a PhD in English, specializing in narrative theories and cognitive literary studies, from the Ohio State University.

Stray Ghazal

cold countries have no gods. blizzards stir a maple or two ever,
to lisp in prayer, cutting through their monotone. ash, cloves and
      ginger

keep us warm. how did we who swore by the sun reach here,
you ask, knee-deep in snow, scratched red by breeze. ash, cloves and
      ginger

diffuse in potions that smell of wooden houses. head down in fire
place, gods who traveled with us turned to ash. cloves and ginger

in every curry you cook, skews my memory. black ice like pepper
tears my skin, blood oozes with saliva. handful of ash, cloves and
      ginger

stain the snow. how will my corpse be cremated in this weather,
you consider—another excuse to not let go? you rub ash, cloves and
        ginger

on my feet and wonder what is acceptable to our gods. bay leaves you
        never put
in rice puddings you served for my birthdays. ash, cloves, ginger

and our lives together resonate with our mispronounced names. return,
        dear,
with me another day to ashen mornings steeped in cloves and ginger.

Kate Hao

Kate Hao is a Chinese poet and fiction writer, a shy Leo, an ex-pianist, a soup enthusiast, an aspiring morning person. Her work has appeared in *Tinderbox Poetry Journal, Cosmonauts Avenue,* and others. She grew up in northern Virginia and currently lives in Providence, Rhode Island.

All I'm Saying Is

No one is better at cracking open a steamed lobster
than my dad is   the shell split along all the right lines
The lobster is heavier than it looks   plastic red
and a lemon slice on top   The lobster is
I would imagine   far from home
My dad only ordered it here because I asked him to
I shouldn't forget my mom and brother   all of us
at a corner table in Maine   by glass and goosebumps
My clam chowder is not really what I had wanted
but my brother suggested it   He's older and says
lobster lungs are not for eating   ocean pollutants
still trapped inside   But I trust my dad as he puts
the best pieces on the edge of my plate and saves none
for himself   Still   I want to check my phone
I want to see the name I want to see   Perhaps
the lobster had a love back in the Atlantic   Another
lobster of similar upbringing   or maybe   a shy mussel?
Somewhere not here   an electric signal via satellite finds home
A screen glows momentary   that knock-knock buzz
The white ladies nearby keep looking at my dad as he eats
My parents leave every plate   clean and I
can only guess why   My clam chowder
is getting cold   My mom wants to hear about my friends

back at school   I feel bad for the lobster
cooked alive in the pot   Outside the window
a stainless steel sky   the cloudy upwards condensation
forming against the stratosphere   I wait for the slow boiling
and the salt to give my end some flavor   I just want
to relate to something   but the lobster must
have had its own lexicon   for ocean
floor   for always never drowning   for the creature
next door with big strange eyes   The lobster
wasn't in the right seminars   never learned the words
queer theory   or   feminist methodologies
and whose fault is that?   My mom takes my bowl
finishes my chowder   and wipes her mouth
She is the only one who still talks with me in Chinese
In Chinese I am a household creature   a domestic
vernacular   I only know how to name what I see at home
By home I mean where I don't get goosebumps
even when the heater breaks   Is the ocean cold
or burning?   I wish the lobster were alive
to tell me   I wish away my secrets pretend
Chinese is my only tongue   Thus everything I hide
disappears   If I don't know how to say something
that means it isn't true   My brother finishes his soup
himself and scrapes the bowl   He asks who I keep texting
I tell all my lies in English   By now the lobster
has been consumed speechless   I'm told
my dad was once an aerospace engineer   precision
his first language   I want to be a formula
a measurable prediction   For every action
there is an equal and extinguishable consequence
To inherit is to combust   I am a timid explosion
No one teaches girls like me to yell   I want
a hunger mouthwatered into love   I want to want
out loud   but we are in Maine   and no one
is speaking   All I'm saying is   dilute

anything enough and eventually it'll be water
again   meaning anything can be made smooth
and necessary   My Chinese is the water   I speak it
and make myself mandatory   Outside the window
Maine is the color of an apple harvest
I want to be grocery shopping   to teach myself
how to pick the ripest fruit   as my mom did
when she first came to this country   She's ready
to go now   having taken napkins for her purse
Wherever we go next   I let all of them decide
like I am a child again   running circles in the kitchen
my mom feeding me apple slices that I let drop to the floor
She bends to pick them up   rinses them at the sink
and   in case they are still dirty   eats them herself
We are walking back to the car to find some new scenery
I trip to keep up   I am always rinsing and making excuses
like   wasn't it just yesterday I left my dinner plates
shining   my saliva the only evidence of a feast?

Mai-Linh K. Hong

Mai-Linh K. Hong writes poetry to explore and make sense of her experiences as an Asian American woman and her family's intergenerational memories of war and migration. She was born in Vietnam and resettled in the United States as a young child. A former lawyer, she is now an English professor who teaches and writes about literature, race, refugees, and justice.

The Road Where My Grandfather Died

A woman folds herself
inside the shade of an orange umbrella

while our driver urges me
to photograph

pavement where *Ông Nội* was
blown to fodder: flesh and
automotive

shrapnel flung
throughout my rented

recollection

        For years I saw
him in the leaf's dash across

my windshield, the punctured
trash bag on the shoulder,

in how such things failed
to explode, how they never launched

bleeding bits of me
to heaven, even if I faltered

on the pedal, even once
stopped traffic in a sudden

dread

      I am older than
He was. His killer, too, no doubt

is dead somewhere. His babes
have grown, scattered, discarded

one another. His eldest, my father
walks the world on varicose legs,

hollow O
of a gun inside his lids,

barbed wire dug into
his writing

hand

      They passed me
their rage and I have lain

spent on roads like this one
in some ragged

lip of mind, chased forgiveness
in pills, running toward the airplane's

shudder, all the while
hurling love like

ballast

    This road, insignificant,
turns up blank on every map

C.X. Hua

C. X. Hua is a poet and artist. She was previously a finalist for the Norman Mailer Award in Poetry, and the winner of the 2019 *Boston Review* Poetry Contest. She has been published or has work forthcoming in *Narrative*, *Boulevard*, and *Electric Lit*.

Green Hills

You asked if the last man
I loved was a woman.
She was a brush
of lipstick
where the red sun
fell into our laps, a bird I shot
into history. Everything felt warm like waiting,
alight with cobwebs, unseen and alive
in their absence. In the countryside,
absence filled entire houses, cut families out
of construction paper, stick figures went missing
on the way to a plate of dinner.
Our house swam up
like a goldfish, asking.
Now, my mother asked
if my father loved men.
Did he love them more than this,
was that it.
He must have loved
a question mark so much
it was no longer allowed by the heart.
Whatever I am allowed makes a memory.
You visit the green hills. They are new every year

like an annual sale, half-off and free. Here
is everything untouched,
please touch
and break and bring
the stranger of your body back home.
You love what will allow itself, sometimes beyond.
Sometimes the sun skips out for days out of searching.
You know there are other homes in the wideness of the low world.

Resi Ibañez

Originally from the northern New Jersey/New York City metro area, Resi Ibañez is a mestiza Filipinx writer and maker who is now based out of Lowell, Massachusetts. They believe in the power of community storytelling to change the world, and have served as a middle school teaching artist, a judge in high school poetry contests, and now as the host of the LGBTQ+ Lowell Open Mic, which they founded. They have been published by *bklyn boihood* and *LOAM* magazine, and will be published in *Atlantic Currents*, a collection of literature joining the cities of Lowell and Cork, Ireland.

The Diaspora According to John Denver

When your mother's going words are
Take me home

When you could not afford the trip
to her burial in Caloocan City
16 hours and oceans and continents away

and all you could listen to
was John Denver's "Take Me Home, Country Roads"[1]
on repeat.

You think of:

how she'd put you on the phone
with titas whose voices come from

home, far away

---

1. Lyrics appearing in this poem are from "Take Me Home,
   Country Roads" by John Denver, 1971

how she'd say "it's already tomorrow over there"
and everything you know about time and place
becomes complicated

life is old there   *older than the trees*

younger than the mountains   *blowing like a breeze*

You think of:
those long road trips.
Eight hours to visit Maryland, Virginia, or Maine
to visit other kids who were mixed like you.

being the first person in your family
to to school in the United States.
when you're asked to write something about home
and you don't know what to say.

You think of:
home.

how Massachusetts is home now,
and was an alternate song lyric:
take me home
to the place
I belong
Massachusetts . . .

You think of:
being homesick for New Jersey,
and the version the New York Knicks used to play:
take me home
to the place
I belong
New York City . . .

You think of:
how New Jersey is not for you.

not anymore.

because your entire sense of self is built on maps
and those sweeping yawns on the steel guitar

the soft beat of finger snaps, foot taps, and a hi-hat
        and how John Denver's echoing voice

becomes your voice now.

in the first song you learned how to play
on those frets with mother-of-pearl inlay

those shells that come from sand and oceans

                                        far far away

take me home

your mother is singing
from a place beyond time and space

You think of:

how you never know what time it is

but you can sing to this tempo
this thrumming rhythm on guitar
a heartbeat echoing through the earth

from tropical Philippine shore to New England shore:

dark and dusty   *painted on the sky*

misty taste of moonshine   *teardrop in my eye*

Dena Igusti

Dena Igusti is an Indonesian Muslim poet, playwright, and journalist based in Queens, New York. She is the co-founder of the multi-disciplinary arts collective UNCOMMON;YOU and the literary press Short Line Review. She is a 2018 NYC Youth Poet Laureate Ambassador and a 2017 Urban Word Federal Hall Fellow. She is a 2019 Player's Theatre Resident Playwright for her co-written Off-Broadway production *Sharum*. She will be an Ars Nova Emerging Leaders Fellow in Spring 2020. Her work has been featured in *BOAAT Press, Peregrine Journal*, and several other publications. She has performed at The Brooklyn Museum, The Apollo Theater, the 2018 Teen Vogue Summit, and several universities across the nation. Her forthcoming collection, *Party Guidelines*, will be published by Game Over Books.

after the incision

felled on a sudden floor in Indonesia // the part that is supposed to be
    my clitoris
expands & bubbles then bubbles & expands // until arms, legs, & a
    head protrude
a figure of flesh, forms what looks // like a body of mine, but the part
    cut out of me still there.

the body leaps across the atlantic // i try to pull it down by the
ankles but
its legs take me with it // we end up in front of my house*
*a plot of brick in the west // i can name home
the body takes the key from my pocket
lets itself in, rushes to my room.

by the time i enter // the body has opened // both closets
rummaged through my things // puts nothing back //

i ask the body *why won't you come back to me?*
the body // scoffs,

                                        why are you hurt?

because you are not mine anymore

the body shrugs its shoulders   *is that the only*
reason you feel loss?
the body takes the shirt we once shared
the photograph of us together //
the underwear we liked //
i tell me *i miss you*

                                    ...

i ask *can we ever happen again*
the body leans in

                                a small pain is
                                        still pain
                                you cut out part of
                                        me
                                do not be
                                surprised that
                                the rest of me left
                                        too

i sob.
i choke out
                i never wanted this.
                they said
                no one could touch us
                if there was nothing to touch
                                i heard another body
                                died from an unwanted
                                        hand
                                the rest of it died shortly
                                        after
                                if i chose the hands
                                that killed the same part
                                i could still live

Ann Inoshita

Ann Inoshita was born and raised on Oʻahu. She earned a Master of Arts degree in English from the University of Hawaiʻi at Mānoa. She is an Assistant Professor at Leeward Community College. She is author of a book of poems, *Mānoa Stream* (Kahuaomānoa Press, 2007), and co-author of linked poetry books, *No Choice but to Follow* (2010) and *What We Must Remember* (2017), both from Bamboo Ridge Press. *What We Must Remember* received the honorable mention for the Ka Palapala Poʻokela award for excellence in literature. She believes poetry must accurately represent people, culture, and places. Every perspective has value including the experiences of Asian American women. Language in various forms should be respected since there is a strong connection between language and culture. She writes in Hawaiʻi Creole English (Pidgin) and standard English.

Japan Trip

My family been hea long time.
I no rememba wen dey wen leave Japan.
We been hea in Hawaiʻi befo statehood—
my bachan wanted us fo visit Japan but,
cuz I neva been dea befo and she wen like
introduce me to da family.

Was one long trip and my body all tired
cuz I stay jetlag.
We visit all da tourist kine place.
I dunno wat dey tink of me.
Dey come up to me and start talking Japanese
den I gotta tell dem wakarimasen.
I no undastand wat dey talking das why.

Remind me of wen I go Waikīkī.
People extra nice to me like dey going sell me someting.
Den wen I open my mouth, dey know I not from Japan
so dey go away.
Eh, maybe I get money, maybe I like buy someting.
Watevas.

We wen go visit my family in da country.
At da house, my bachan wen drop to da floor
and bow so low I neva know wat fo do.
I just standing on da side in my jeans and I feel so stupid.
I no like insult nobody and I dunno wat fo do.
My bachan start talking Japanese and I dunno wat she talking.

Mo betta if I wen pay mo attention afta elementary school
wen I used to go to da Honwanji mission fo learn Japanese.
Hard fo study Japanese, but wen you like be like everybody else
and nobody talking Japanese.

Look like my bachan explaining someting.
Everybody stay nodding and smiling at me.
Ho, good ting man.

Weird, yeah. I know how fo be in my house
but I dunno wat fo do hea.

Sometime hard fo be Local.
Sometime hard fo be American.
And sometime hard fo be Japanese.

Sometime I feel like I no belong no place.
I wonda if people tink befo dey come stay Hawai'i.
Hawai'i good but I know I wen lose someting.
Hard fo go back.

Doyali Islam

Doyali Islam was a Griffin Poetry Prize finalist for her second book, *heft* (McClelland & Stewart, 2019). Doyali has participated in CBC Books' *Why I Write* video-interview series. She has discussed the value of silence on CBC Radio's *The Sunday Edition*; language, form, beauty, and empathy with Anne Michaels in *CV2*; and the relationship between poetry and the body on CBC Radio's *The Next Chapter*. In an *Adroit Journal* conversation with Forrest Gander, Doyali has said: "I want to survive. I want my readers-listeners to survive. I want certain kinds of language to survive. I want certain versions of history to survive. I want questions to survive." Doyali understands writing/reading poetry as a physical practice based in whole-body listening – an act/art of trespass and kinship – and empathy as vital to craft. Of Bangladeshi and Arab ancestry, she lives in Canada.

water for canaries
july 26, 2014

the a.p. photo shows two men of beit
hanoun. during the ceasefire, they had gone
back to what they called home to find their
birds alive amid debris. one pours with fraught
hands from a bottle: it's a small-throated
mercy, surviving a strike from the air.
but which photo can recall the deft

quiet fusing of clavicles into
one auspicious fork—bones hollowing—the
sprout of feathers—? no memory of the long
flight into their bodies—the last singing
descendants of a burning world—the first
heirs of a new, they preen in their pink cage.
their bodies emanate fine clouds of dust.

light

april 7, 2017

standing on a plastic stool, my father
changes the bulb in the ceiling fixture
in the den. having aged, he no longer
    bothers to dress; lives in sets of pjs
that sheathe him in diamond-like patterns. still,
    the rigour of a former engineer:
each twist staccato and measured until
edison screw cap comes loose from socket.
my vantage point is from below: from here,
    scarlet shells flutter down through dim
air – last repose discarded with the lamp.
they died in their quest for warmth, but others
camp – set up homes in the room's wide corners.
    the man is no saint but with moth,
        spider, ant, or beetle he is tender
as an underarm revealed through repair;
his *den*, a true *denn* (old english for lair).
    maybe for him it is easier to love
what is not his by blood, what seeks only
        passage or refuge.

tonight, he works quietly while the tv
conjectures: *what is to come* (more hunger,
danger) *for the syrian people?* his
pjs, amid the garish sound bites, seem
patterned not with diamond but with missile
crosshairs,

        |
    ------ ------
        |

        tracking and targeting a land
not his own. ladybird and tomahawk
have both rained down, and bbc *waits for dust
to settle*—speaks in the interim of
crisis, risk. my father listens but reaches
beyond full height—one hand closed around
a new bulb. i see him as counterpoise:
left arm, slack; right arm, raised; right hand, a fist:
silhouetted in doubled dark, he is
intent on his chore—until the light,
the light is restored.

Bhanu Kapil

Bhanu Kapil was born in the United Kingdom and lives in the United States and the United Kingdom. She is the author of a number of full-length works of poetry/prose, including *The Vertical Interrogation of Strangers* (Kelsey Street Press, 2001), *Incubation: a space for monsters* (Leon Works, 2006), *humanimal [a project for future children]* (Kelsey Street Press, 2009), *Schizophrene* (Nightboat, 2011), *Ban en Banlieue* (Nightboat, 2015), and *How to Wash a Heart* (Liverpool University Press, 2020). Kapil received the Windham Campbell Prize for Poetry in 2020. She teaches at Naropa University and in Goddard College's low-residency MFA program.

Advice from My Great-Grandmother: Poem for the Daughter I Never Had

Avoid spaces in which white people you don't know congregate.

[Sorry, but that's the end of the poem. It's the last day of May ***, and it's the only thing I need you to know. Don't worry. The other stuff is there. In my notebook, I've scrawled the recipe for saag* and a remedy for menstrual pain**, in the long tradition of instructions passed verbally within a family until they reach the descendant. Can a ghost be a descendant****? What happened to your blood? Who drained you off?]

*Add a tablespoon of red lentils.

**Blue cohosh, vitex, nettle, valerian root, motherwort, boiled to a simmer then strained.

A month of carnage and ambivalence, characterized by the prevailing belief that whiteness confers a kind of greatness. The imperial category was both acute and weak in the first six months of 2020. We snapped it in two but it tripled, evoking a bygone past. We noticed, also, that it wanted its own comfort* at all costs, and that when comfort was denied, it froze to a high sheen. That sheen was a wet mirror. It absorbed and deflected any glare. "I was protecting my wife and child from certain violence," said whiteness. And: "I did nothing wrong."

****Kenneth Jones and Tema Okun: "The belief that those with power have a right to emotional and psychological comfort; scapegoating those who cause discomfort; equating individual acts of unfairness against white people with systemic racism which daily targets people of color."

Avid, precise, murderous.

The syllabus, once a radical category, was out there more than it was in here.

In the world you live in, I'm not sure if there are universities, or a country called The United States, or another country, The United Kingdom.

Daughter, this is a poem and so I'm sending you my courage.

And I'm sending you my love.

What I know of your great-great-great grandmother is this:

Under British rule, she wove a hemp rug dyed with berries and other natural things.

On this rug was a leopard.

The leopard was wearing a diamond choker.

A bloody tongue poking out.

Goodnight, said the leopard, a word stitched vertically in front of its face.

Can you discern it?

Goodnight, Empire.

Goodnight, white supremacy.

Your veins are dangling from my teeth.

Maya Khosla

Maya Khosla is a wildlife biologist and writer. She served as the Poet Laureate of Sonoma County (2018-2020), bringing Sonoma's communities together for a filmed reading series, the Legacy Project. She was born in the United Kingdom, raised there and in India, Bhutan, and Myanmar, places that continue to inform her work. Trained in the biological sciences, the wild grounds her writing – most recently, thousands of field hours spent in untouched post-fire forests that grow full of life. Her books include *All the Fires of Wind and Light* (Sixteen Rivers Press, 2019), *Keel Bone* (Dorothy Brunsman Poetry Prize from Bear Star Press, 2003), and *Heart of the Tearing*, (Red Dust Press, 1996). In 2020 she won the PEN Oakland / Josephine Miles Award for *All the Fires of Wind and Light*. Her poems have been featured in documentary films, nominated for Pushcart Prizes and featured in *River Teeth, Poem*, and other journals. Her short film projects have been supported by organizations including Patagonia, Environment Now, and Creative Sonoma.

Lemon Tree

We gather the way we have done
for years, a semicircle or sometimes
a full circle in ashy darkness
and well-watered soil underfoot,
leaves brushing against cheeks, lights
from your home and other lives
spilling down so the top leaves
glint and this internal country, a tracery
of roadways bound by bark, this country
of hopeful undulations, is showing itself
as a being that keeps carrying water
toward lanterns full lemon-yellow light.

Each of us stands at the edge
of a personal darkness, we test the weight
of each globe; one of us fills her pockets,
another a bag, another the baggy space
in a stretched sweater, and the lanterns
in this tree speak no language and speak
of brightness and change, and no matter
what we do with them, whether we sprinkle
their transparent fluids on steaming fish
or blend the lemons, skin and all
with blueberries, we will continue
to carry the darkness, the sweet
and bitter-sour sense of hope, into our days.

Maddie Kim

Maddie Kim is a Korean American writer from Los Angeles. Her work has appeared in the Asian American Writers' Workshop's *The Margins, Tinderbox Poetry Journal, The Journal,* and *The Adroit Journal,* among others. She is an incoming PhD student in English literature whose research centers on Asian American art and literature's relationships to historical memory, racialized embodiment, and performance.

Letter to My Ancestors

The blue buckets on the shower floor were useless
against the drought. I dismembered the hydrangeas
in the garden and put them in my dress pockets.
I left my mother's house. I crossed the deadened brush
along the highway where the unclothed body of a woman
was once found by the headlights of two teenagers.
I dropped a trail of hydrangea heads like a crop circle
in the dust. This is how Seoul must have looked: dark patches
of village soil covering kimchi jars buried in even rows.
Except here three generations of time have made barren
the wilderness of what birthed me. I looked for a body
but instead found the entire landscape a grave: the cashier
at the grocery shoving my pears into plastic, the man
on the phone trying to sell me a house with no windows.
During the Joseon dynasty women fortunate enough
to bear sons flaunted their breasts in crowded village markets.
When I learned this I held my mother's backyard oranges
silently to my chest, dreamt of rice paddies draining
from the highest terrace. Grains arched and shivering.
Weary as the oar risen from the river. Ancestors, tell me
where you have collected the water which from its blade
has ascended. I want to return to that other life.

How I Wait for You to Return from Your Naturalization Ceremony

I have covered the rungs of the stepladder in palm oil
so that now I must jump onto the bed with a running start
like a Portuguese water dog, which, days before Bo was born
in Texas, I desperately wanted the Obama family to choose.
You were a fifth grader living in Korea then, so I recreate
my fifth grade *Scholastic* magazine poll with a blue pen
into the sheets. Then I empty the desk drawer of its boarding passes
and receipts, covering every paper surface with the alphabet
I asked you to teach me on those first dates in Thai restaurants
and in the dim light of my bedroom after waking, because
as children when my mother said *jury* instead of *jewelry*
my brother and I laughed at her until she cried, her legs
tucked underneath her in the passenger seat. I write over and over
the fifteen hangul vowels I cannot pronounce, their romanizations
tacked onto hyphens like tails: *eoh, weuh, oui.* Tonight, when you
return, you will be an American and I will still be a girl who needs
a translator to read in my mother's language, my mouth full
of so few shapes. I fall into the habits of my mother, it's true.
I walk to the store repeating to myself impossible sounds,
and in the soap aisle I pretend to look for soap. Tonight,
after driving you home from the airport, I will show you all
the possibilities I have laid out on the bed: soft-coated Wheaten
     Terrier,
Bichon Frise, Labradoodle. I will ask you to call me *Sunmi*, the name
my mother gave me. It means *beautiful declaration.* I wear it shyly
like an invisible ring. I used to be so quiet the first grade teacher
with the chair at the front of the room believed I needed to be
     frightened
in order to speak. But do you remember how we met in the basement
of a house party, your aloneness compelling me to ask about the
     language

of your mother, even though I already knew? Tonight, before we curl
into bed, I will ask you, new citizen, to fold my dresses into squares
like tiny flags so that when I wear them I will look like a girl inside
a grid: linen creases forming the strokes of the hangul vowels
my mother never taught me, believing that every daughter
who was wanted was given an impossible name.

Juliet S. Kono

Juliet S. Kono was born in 1943, and raised in Hilo, Hawai'i. She is a survivor of the 1946 tsunami. She has written extensively about the Japanese American experience across the generations. Using narrative and poetic styles, she seeks to give voice to those who would have otherwise faded into oblivion. She especially wants to give voice to the women immigrants who came to Hawai'i as contract laborers. She is the author of two books of poetry, *Hilo Rains* and *Tsunami Years*, a short story collection, *Ho'olulu Park and the Pepsodent Smile*, and most notably, *Anshū*, a novel. She is presently working on another novel, *Misao's Body*. She is a recipient of the Hawai'i Award for Literature, American Japanese National Literary Award, and the US/ Japan Friendship Commission Creative Artist Exchange Fellowship.

Nowhere

1.
I began my walk in the newer part
of the garden—built during the Meiji *jidai*,

my grandmother's era—through a moss
trail shaded by a canopy of maple trees turning

color that cuts away to a stone path
of rounded, softly gray pond pebbles, darkening

in the quiet rain, in spots at first,
then over them in a shallow water's spread

after the downpour. She always wanted
to go back to Japan, see a garden like this once more.

2.
Ahead, at the end of the trail stood
a massive lichen-covered boulder, obstructing

what was ahead until I rounded it. I gasped
when the land opened its curtain to a view of a large pond

with its spine of stepping stones and a wooden
bridge spanning toward a small island with a *matsu* tree,

wired and staked into shape, three large
basalt boulders standing guard. The dark pond reflected

white clouds sweeping overhead and all
was quiet when the rain stopped. Sagging lotus stems

and leaves drooped near a bank, looking like
upside down umbrellas on the pond's still surface.

This, all of this.

3.
All her life, she talked crazily about going home. Far off,
I could hear the qua qua of crows, as if they were laughing at her
        notion.

She finally made a trip to where her need resided.
Quickly found she could not hold onto the pond, its rocks and water,

the pines, the sky, the mountains of silence.
Everything slipping away, she found she belonged nowhere—

neither from where she had come from
nor where she had gone to—boundaries no longer existing.

A picture of her in the tour group from Hawaiʻi tells it all.
Her holding a small tourist's white-locater flag, as if in surrender,
        her face

long and weary. She got sick after she came home; things never the
        same.

Hyejung Kook

Hyejung Kook was born in Seoul, grew up in Pennsylvania, and now lives in Kansas with her husband and their two children. Her work has recently appeared in *Pleiades*, *The World I Leave You: Asian American Poets on Faith and Spirit*, *The Massachusetts Review*, and *Glass: A Journal of Poetry*. She is a Fulbright grantee and a Kundiman fellow. She sees poetry as a call to attend, to be open, and to use all her resources to make sense of the world and thus create new worlds. She is often guided by the physicality of language, the way words move through her and the air and on the page. Having children has deepened her understanding of attention, of how it imparts value and power, and also has reinforced how all writing is political, emanating from a body in relation to the polis, and that hers is Korean American and female.

The Day Dr. Christine Blasey Ford Testifies Before the Senate Judiciary Committee, I Teach My Daughter the Names of the Parts of Female Anatomy

Today we have naming of parts. Yesterday,
in the park, you shrieked, *my butt, my butt hurts*,
after a little sand had worked its way into your
labial folds. Your two-year-old voice piercing
as a hawk's. I held you open
in bright sunlight to make sure I removed every
tiny grain as you whimpered and flinched
no matter how gentle I tried to be. *I don't
have all the answers*, but when you ask today,
I have these names at least to give you.

Today we have naming of parts. And tomorrow,
you will chant the words over and over in the way
of toddlers, entranced by repetition. But today

we have naming of parts. This is the labia,
where the sand hurt you yesterday. The labia
protects the vagina, where when you are older,
blood will come out once a month, like the full moon
you love. It doesn't hurt to bleed like this.
The vagina is also where babies come out.
Where you came out.

A ring of fire
before the circlet
of my flesh tore
just a little
just one stitch
needed to hold me
together again

When I was young, maybe five or six—*I don't remember
as much as I would like to*—two older boys shoved
sand down my underwear. I stood, shocked,
then began to cry for the shame and then the hurt
when I tried to walk. *Indelible in the hippocampus is
the laughter* while I hobbled, bow-legged,
trying to lessen the pain of the grit
between my legs. I didn't know the word *labia* then.
I didn't tell my mother what happened.

Yes, I believe
it was a sunny day.
Or was it cloudy?
But I am
one hundred percent
certain grape hyacinth
bloomed beside the swings.

Today we have naming of parts. This is the urethra,
where pee comes out. And this is the anus,
where poop comes out. Here is the clitoris.
It feels good to touch. No one else should
be touching you in these places except
family while cleaning you or a doctor
checking if you are hurt.

> *I am here today not*
> *because I want to be.*
>
> *I am here because*
> *I believe it is my civic duty*
> *to tell you*
>
> *the truth*

Today we have naming of parts.
This is not a flower. This is not a peach.
This is the labia. This is the vagina.
Not the sheath of an ear of grain.
This is the clitoris. Not a key nor
a little hill. This is the urethra.
This is the anus. The parts are yours.
The names, yours.

This is my wish.
The power of true names,
capable of binding, a circle
of protection, these words a ward
in your little girl voice, the sweet
and singsong lilt as you try each
sound, make what I believed

unlovely lovely, charming,
a charm against evil.

> *I am here because*
> I cannot hold you
> within the circle
> of myself the way
> I once did our edges
> blurred you broke
> free shrieking
> fierce little eyes
> don't let them
> break you you
> are here *I am*
> *here* we will
> utter the truth
> of ourselves

For today we have naming of parts.

*Italicized portions are quotations from Dr. Christine Blasey
Ford's testimony to the Senate Judiciary Committee,
September 27, 2018.

Larissa Lai

Larissa Lai has authored three novels, *The Tiger Flu* (Arsenal Pulp, 2018), *Salt Fish Girl* (Thomas Allen, 2002) and *When Fox Is a Thousand* (Press Gang, 1995); three poetry books, *sybil unrest* (with Rita Wong) (New Star, 2013), *Automaton Biographies* (Arsenal Pulp, 2009), and *Iron Goddess of Mercy* (Arsenal Pulp, 2021); a chapbook, *Eggs in the Basement* (Nomados, 2009); and a critical book, *Slanting I, Imagining We: Asian Canadian Literary Production in the 1980s and 1990s* (Wilfrid Laurier University Press, 2014). A recipient of the Astraea Foundation Emerging Writers' Award, and a finalist for seven others, she holds a Canada Research Chair at the University of Calgary, where she directs The Insurgent Architects' House for Creative Writing.

Dear Bodhisattva

Dear Bodhisattva, our administration denies your application requests further documentation on the relations of your emanations rendering dubious the station of your creation. We need fists to prove this. We need fish, we need bones, a pound of mesh, the behest of the donor laying kroner on the holler of your partial dollar. We need fodder for our error. We'll take your tribute, your mother, your father, a grist of sisters and your heart and liver to luck our buck, clean the hands of our boys their pleasures and ploys are the first ducks in our row. Your attitude of beatitude belies ingratitude to the ones who died for the sins they pinned on you. Blue? Achoo! Your allergy's a cover for the coven roasting witches we hunted to make the world spin the other way round. Have your say. We'll listen to the first sentence substituting every noun for a clown in brown make-up, take up every connotation for our own elation. The conflagration doesn't want to talk about a past that doesn't serve it soft as a futon for our loft or ice cream at the take out with strawberry sauce. Lay your lubber on the tracks of the

hack cracking codes to keep what we have under wraps. We'll stack
your vertebrae backwards to slow your cerebral progress through dense
biscuits of empty carbs, while we lark on a wing of our own narking,
build more parking for CEOS and fund managers while you bandage
what's bleeding. We gotta keep on feeding, it's how we're leading in the
polls for trolls. Stow your eggroll til you've grown more beansprouts,
grouted the wall we've built to keep you out and double-glazed the
glass ceiling. Once more, with feeling! We want you reeling the blud-
geon of fake news til the truth makes you stupid, caught in the loop
of chasing the tail we pinned on your donkey. Had enough, you're
through? Here's a revolving door to take your exit, all the world's a gage
of how we'll measure you by a yardstick turned to beepers doubling
down on the best bloopers we lifted from the stone of your phone.
Don't groan, your loan's overdue and accumulating interest in the al-
gorithm of our decision, baking lesions deep in the meat of your liver.
We'll peck it out for you at good price, calculated in rice, be nice and
we'll throw in an eagle for free.

Sister Rita

Hawks a gob

Scoffs at toffs   sips duck congee

Amy Lam

Amy Lam is a writer and editor based in Portland, Oregon. She is a Kundiman fellow and has been awarded scholarships from the Fine Arts Work Center, Napa Valley Writers' Conference, an artist residency at Loghaven, and was an alumna of the Tin House Summer Workshop. Her work has appeared and is forthcoming in *Tin House*, *Gay Mag*, *Indiana Review*, and more.

Autobiography of a mouth

There are no rewards for your body doing what it's supposed to do. I hid my baby teeth anyway. Hoping the small pebble beneath my pillow would turn into a dollar bill. Ran my tongue across metallic gums. Dedi said I laugh too loud. I swallowed his admonishment whole and laughed from below my belly until his words came up from behind my throat and jumped out a shriek. A-mah was an unhappy old woman. She sat in Uncle's house all day sipping on a can of lukewarm Budweiser. Told me my two front teeth were wrong. I said nothing in return, no talking back. My words would have been a hot breath with no sound. She died, we wore white, I got braces, forgave her. Inherited Ma's mouth in name only, because I am her only daughter. She says my lips, thick and defiant, are nothing like hers. I grew a tongue of my own for she had none to pass onto me. My jaw speaks to itself at night. Grind, gnash, snap. My skull is a witness as I sleep. As if enough pressure could turn my molar into a three-carat emerald cut diamond.

Devi S. Laskar

Devi S. Laskar is a poet and photographer, and author of *The Atlas of Reds and Blues*, a critically acclaimed novel that grapples with racism, misogyny, and being invisible in America. A native Tar Heel, Ms. Laskar now lives in California with her family.

The Fear I Walk Around

after Jessica Greenbaum's "The Yellow Star that Goes with Me"

Sometimes I hold it the way I hold my head in the mornings.
Sometimes I wrestle it like a teenage boy who's won trophies
     and is liked at school.
Sometimes I duck it in the alley outside my doctor's office
but it turns up, it always turns up, like my shadow a moment
     later.

Sometimes I could win trophies, remember being liked at
     school by a teenage boy.
Sometimes it is hard to breathe, not because the air is foul but
     because it is familiar and sweet.
It turns up, it always turns up, like my shadow a moment later,
     but
no one gives me chocolates or a ticker tape parade for trying to
     outrun it.

Sometimes it is hard to breathe, not because the air is foul but
     because it is familiar and sweet.
When I am a boy I am camping in the wilderness and mourning
     the loss of my father though he is still alive and though
     he still knows my name.
No one gives me chocolates or a ticker tape parade for trying to
     outrun it.

Sometimes it wants me to treat it like a lover, but I always see
     it as trench-coat-wearing exhibitionist that it really is.

When I am a boy I am camping in the wilderness and mourning
     the loss of my father though he is still alive and though
     he still knows my name.
When I am a girl, I'm an old girl, as in the horse with three
     foals, a horse penned in to a decaying meadow, rotting
     because of the landfill lesser men have planted below
     the surface generations ago.
Sometimes it wants me to treat it like a lover, but I always see
     it as a trench-coat-wearing exhibitionist that it really is.
Sometimes I ignore it and travel light, continue to eat street
     food from umbrella-sheltered carts though the vendor is
     giving me stink eye, and I think about the future.
When I am a girl, I'm an old girl, as in the horse with three
     foals, a horse penned into a decaying meadow, rotting
     because of the landfill lesser men have planted below
     the surface generations ago.
When I'm an older man, I always remember to call my mother
     on Sundays.

Sometimes I ignore it and travel light, continue to eat street
     food from umbrella-sheltered carts though the vendor is
     giving me stink eye, and I think about the future.
Sometimes I am optimistic when I don't hear it knocking on
     the back door for five consecutive minutes, an insistent
     sound like the woodpecker or the caw of a hungry
     crow.

When I'm an older man, I always remember to call my mother
     on Sundays.
When I am a middle-aged woman, I'm standing in my
     driveway and the policeman is pointing his weapon at
     my head.

Sometimes I am optimistic when I don't hear it knocking on
the back door for five consecutive minutes, an insistent
sound like the woodpecker or the caw of a hungry
crow.
Sometimes I pretend to be a colicky infant strapped to a car-
seat being driven around at night.

When I am a middle-aged woman, I'm standing in my
driveway and the policeman is pointing his weapon at
my head.
When I am a middle-aged woman, and I am almost always a
middle-aged woman, the woman on her driveway is
someone I know well, and in the policeman's hand is an
assault rifle.
Sometimes I pretend to be a colicky infant strapped to a car-
seat being driven around at night.
It doesn't matter if it's the first Thursday in November or the
third Monday in May, it knows the date and time of
day, it knows where to find me.

When I am a middle-aged woman, and I am almost always a
middle-aged woman, the woman on her driveway is
someone I know well, and in the policeman's hand is an
assault rifle.
Sometimes I duck it in the alley outside my doctor's office.
It doesn't matter if it's the first Thursday in November or the
third Monday in May, it knows the date and time of
day, it knows where to find me.
Sometimes I hold it the way I hold my head in the mornings.

Iris A. Law

Iris A. Law is a Kundiman fellow, author of the chapbook *Periodicity* (Finishing Line Press, 2013), and founding coeditor of the literary magazine *Lantern Review: A Journal of Asian American Poetry*. Her work has been published in numerous literary journals, has twice been nominated for a Pushcart Prize, and was selected for Best of the Net in 2009. Born and raised in southern New Jersey, Iris received her MFA from the University of Notre Dame and now lives and writes in the San Francisco Bay Area.

Cho Chang in the Storm

How much I wanted it—to be split clean as if
by viridian lightning, bright truth slicking my path
as I stumbled among the rocks.

They laughed at me for striding
into the thunderstruck night.
But I wanted its noise and the wet of it,

the jagged, black fingers of water
raking the blood to the surface of my skin.
I knew I could not have called him back.

I remembered the wound's white stink,
singed flesh that unsprang its glistening edge
in me. How I longed to run my hands against

that bruise-colored sky, to swallow
the sinewy clouds, their damp notes
of iron and earth. *Let me just taste,*

I thought, and I curled my lips around
jam-thick dark, sliced free the spine
of the moor with my tongue. It was warm.

Its fat squidged. I grew wilder.
Let me lick it clean, I thought.
Let me fondle the bones with my teeth.

Cut Pieces

In the ICU my mother sits shaking,
a pair of wire cutters in her hands
and a plastic zip bag clutched to her chest.
She has just cut my father's wedding ring
from his finger. *Now,* she said to the nurse,
and the young woman helped her snip
the last thirty years of her life in two.

The Christmas I was sixteen, we woke
to a soft, startled drumming in the garage.
My father opened the door to find a small,
brown bird, its wings stuck fast to a glue trap
meant for rodents, beating itself against
the concrete in a fluster of feathers and blood.

Gently, he gathered the panicked creature
into a bath towel. He snipped the paper and glue
from around its wings and feet and then, to wait
out the storm, placed it in a greenhouse box,
where it threw itself against the glass sides
until its heart stopped and its body was still.

In the waiting room, I watch my mother
fold in on herself. Her shoulder blades quake
beneath the bright red hump of her sweater.
He's free now, she says, and *what else could I do*—
over and over, but she cannot will her fist to open,
her hand to release the cut pieces of that which she'd said
she would have and would hold.

Jenna Le

Jenna Le is a daughter of Vietnamese refugees born and raised just outside Minneapolis. She holds a BA in mathematics and an MD and works as a physician and educator. Her poetry collections are *Six Rivers* (NYQ Books, 2011) and *A History of the Cetacean American Diaspora* (Anchor & Plume, 2016), the latter of which won Second Place in the 2017 Elgin Awards. She was selected by Marilyn Nelson as winner of Poetry by the Sea's inaugural sonnet competition and also has recent poems in *AGNI, Poet Lore,* and *West Branch.* In her poetry, she strives to make something new out of traditional poetic forms in a way that engages the imagination and emotions, while honoring perspectives that have been underrepresented in English-language poetry.

Purses

in memoriam Kate Spade

When our Quiz Bowl team of eighteen-year-olds snagged
　　　　a berth in the finals, held in New York City,

　　　　my small-town Minnesotan brain cells dizzied—
at last I'd be some place that *mattered.* Swag

was my teammate Anne's fixation: knockoff bags
　　　　peddled in Chinatown, affixed with glitzy

　　　　Kate Spade labels. Anne bought a sack of six,
then forgot it on the airport shuttle's shag

seats; someone swiped it within minutes. Kate,
　　　　I learned a fact of womanhood that year:

even we knockoff girls, cheap, desperate
to look like someone else, to imitate

      a finer woman, have our value; we're
      wanted, wanted, until we disappear.

Epicenter Thoughts

Note: Since the COVID-19 epidemic reached the United States, hate incidents directed against Asian Americans have risen, and continue to rise, dramatically.

I'm wary, now, of going out alone,
Dear. What unnerves me more about train rides:
the virus, or the risk of being thrown
against the train car's floor or seats or sides

by someone yelling hate, like what befell
a gray-haired man in my own neighborhood
three weeks ago, when fears had yet to swell
up to their present height? Back in the "good

old days," I had at times already sensed
my cidery skin tone caused me to be read
as interloper: a girl made threats against
me at the laundromat because (she said)

my "smell" offended her—that was last fall—
and how could things not be worse now this virus
fuels people's fervor to erect a wall
around the things they care about, desirous

of saving what they can when poverty,
inequity are menacing their children?
Days prior, as I hurried down the three
blocks stretched between a pair of clinic buildings,

I thought: might it protect me if I wore
my hospital I.D. outside my jacket,
displayed with ostentation? That might score
me some reprieve—but others would still lack it.

Karen An-hwei Lee

A daughter of immigrants, Karen An-hwei Lee is a Taiwanese American whose poetry, prose, and translations dwell at the interstices of her faith journey, bicoastal landscapes, and postcolonial/feminist frameworks. A recipient of an NEA grant, she holds degrees from Brown University and the University of California, Berkeley. Born and raised in New England, she currently divides her time between Seattle and San Diego. Her recent books are *The Maze of Transparencies* (Ellipsis, 2019), *Sonata in K* (Ellipsis, 2016), and *Phyla of Joy* (Tupelo, 2012).

On the Levitation of Beautiful Objects

For those millennials who desire one, here is a tale. Once upon a lifetime, in my turbulent years as a weather system, I was a typhoon named Karen. If I whirled my spiral rainbands in the north, my rotation would've shifted to the right. In reality, the Coriolis Effect deflected my movement in the southern hemisphere.

A corrective footnote in meteorological history, for the record—

I made landfall as a tropical storm, not a hurricane
      by the Isla de la Juventad, the Isle of Youth. On
        this archipelago, I alighted on an isle,
     kissed the gangly mangrove shores,
       upset ferries, hydrofoils, yachts.

While serenity blew a puff of air – a glaucoma test in my solo eye – I roared no to sea ports and unreeled an archive of 35 mm film, no to fashion institutes, no to civil engineering, no to female pelvic exams, no to forced sterilization, no to acid vibes of the bay, absolutely no to war, a decolonial no to imperialism. A thousand megawatts powering a million off-shore turbines,

I tossed a love note into my namesake storm—
Dear brazen fury of *juventad*, I lost strength while
summoning the beauty of the unanchored, not the lost.
Pure verticality and relentless power, as the world's rudest
tambourine, I dragged my inclemency over palmetto
groves, fishing piers, and utility lines. Beloved denizens of
the archipelago, so very anthropocentric in scope, you
failed to see

  I was only levitating beautiful objects.

Michelle Lee

Michelle Lee is a Korean American writer interested in exploring the different and complicated ideas associated with home. She earned her BA in English Creative Writing and Women's & Gender Studies from Wells College and her MFA in Writing for Children and Young Adults from the New School. She lives in unceded Lenape territory known as Manhattan and works in children's publishing.

how to bake bread

gather a stone from all fifty states
bottle storm water from the shore
hold the salty sea breeze in your
alveoli while counting the steps
from here to there take that
number and divide by the years
by the days by the hours you
have waited in a house built
out of birch wood where you have
answered every telemarketer to
build good credit with the universe
taken in the stray spiders swaying
in windows placed them on looms half-
strung with yarn made from your mother's
mother's silver hair unleash the
breath molding in your lungs
when you lay tonight under a
patchwork roof stare at the glare
of the moon and whisper all the
secrets curdled in the lining of
your skin making muck
out of your veins.

Mari L'Esperance

Mari L'Esperance was born in Kobe, Japan, to a Japanese mother and a French Canadian-New Englander father and raised in Southern California, Guam, and Japan. A graduate of New York University's Creative Writing Program, L'Esperance is the author of *The Darkened Temple* (University of Nebraska Press, 2008), winner of the Prairie Schooner Book Prize in Poetry, and co-editor (with Tomás Q. Morín) of *Coming Close: Forty Essays on Philip Levine* (Prairie Lights Books/ University of Iowa Press, 2013). She is also the author of *Begin Here*, winner of the 2000 Sarasota Poetry Theatre Press Chapbook Prize. The recipient of awards and residencies from the *New York Times*, New York University, Djerassi Resident Artists Program, Hedgebrook, and Dorland Mountain Arts Colony, L'Esperance lives in the San Francisco Bay Area.

Anju, from the Far World

after seven paintings by Fuyuko Matsui

Ringed tracery
on the lake's face
is what you saw,
but you were wrong
to assume. Forgive me,

but drowning's not
my thing. While
you knelt in the weeds,
weeping, I slipped
through the trees. Here

I recede to dun, beetles
and leaf mold

my familiars. Here
I take my leave, my Bereaved.
My Afflictions.

*

In blue-black woods,
it appeared to me, cold
and primordial.

Dear Other, Dear Shadow,
I'm done for—a tracery
in red on black.

*

All's not what it seems.
There's a story here:
ghost of my brother fled
in my stead, our
mother mere memory—

*

There's a story here:
tracery of hair snared
in the branches—black
branches lacing the air—

dank odor of lake water,
scrap of song wafting
across the sound
from Sado-ga-shima—

*

Deliver me, wind
in the pines—pitch
dark—shrieks
of night birds—

Deliver me, white
Narcissus spent to ash.

I'm undone.
I'll never come clean.

Nancy Chen Long

Nancy Chen Long is a poet of Taiwanese and American descent. Her poetry tends to explore the nooks and crannies at the intersections of science, art, and religion. She is the author of *Wider than the Sky* (Diode Editions, 2020), which was chosen for the Diode Editions Book Award, and *Light into Bodies* (University of Tampa Press, 2017), winner of the Tampa Review Prize for Poetry. She was awarded a National Endowment of the Arts Creative Writing Fellowship and a writers' residency at Ox-Bow School of the Arts. Her work was selected as the winner of the Poetry Society of America Robert H. Winner Award and featured in *Poetry Daily, Verse Daily,* and *Indiana Humanities*. Recent poems can be found in *Copper Nickel, The Southern Review,* and *The Cincinnati Review*.

Why There Is No Interest in Singing

In these times of heave and eddy,
the people have grown

austere. Brambles should have caught flame
by now. A reluctant warrior should have emerged

to orate forth an opus. Home is where the psalm is
and so I choral my offspring as I am able,

encourage them to emote their own opera,
compose a truth—some chord of code, perhaps a hex

in A minor, one not locked into that logic
of the common meter.

My young dutifully mouth the sanctioned libretto.
Their syncopated arrangements are an alien strain

unwelcome in the standard repertoire.
They cannot outshout the refrain

that programs them to whitewash. To be an asset
in today's troupe demands a singer

eschew all appearances
of singing. Improvisation invites discord—

so many more doorkeepers now.
The homeland beats with a wind-bluffed,

boot-strapped people
who like every boot to be on the ground, to die

with their boots on.
A call to voice is a call to asphyxiation.

Too soon song will be roped
into the service of boots,

useful only as cadence, a tool to control
the neighborhood troops in a war march.

Angie Sijun Lou

Angie Sijun Lou is a Kundiman Fellow and a PhD candidate in Literature and Creative Writing at the University of California, Santa Cruz.

Ritual Warfare

I left my window open all night & now rain

gushes in my bedroom as if through two milk-white

teeth. I look outside and witness another year

growing around a tree, the ring engraved on its bones,

strangely lit. A long time ago, I was told of shamans

carving oracles in the shoulder blades of oxen,

the diligence in which they heated bones

& deciphered etchings, squinting under pale

light. You say you hate the mole living

on your upper lip, the next evening I witness you

carve it out with a razorblade. It's strange how we

knife up magnolias, force them

into bloom, how we can no longer wait

for real gods to come slice us open. Already I've forgotten

my past incarnations. We fall asleep with the lights

on. You put your head in my palms the way

a tree (thunder-charred), refuses to reveal

how it became dead

& still empties itself for my touch.

Pacyinz Lyfoung

Pacyinz Lyfoung is a French-born, Minnesota-grown, 1.5 Hmong American woman poet. Her love of reading started as a little French girl devouring the "Oui-Oui" books that she begged her parents to buy. She came to poetry to meet two needs: she sought the power of poetry to 1) reach across social divides and 2) celebrate her family and cultural heritage and preserve their histories. She has studied poetry at the Loft, VONA, Winter Tangerine, the George Washington University Jenny McKean Moore Community Poetry Workshop, and at Split This Rock. She currently works as a consultant at the intersection of intellectual property and innovations in the arts and technology. She most recently published poems in Split This Rock's *The Quarry: A Social Justice Poetry Database* and in the *Stonecoast Review*.

Morning Radio

My mother switches on the TV
moving pots and pans
warming up bread
and making coffee
she does not watch the images
without images
the news and ad jingles stream
like a radio show
like back in the days in her old country
where farmers and their wives in remote villages
kept track of the war and political rollercoasters
in a nation in transition
on top of mountains beneath the clouds
amidst the rice fields
and the squash flowers dangling
from the corn rows

the voices from somewhere else
talk of things that can't seem real
until they suddenly screech or
worse yet, become dead silent
and there is no need for images
to know bombs will drop
if not here,
somewhere close to here
already too close to here
in her kitchen half a world away
half a life away
on another morn of a new life
the sound of the TV
buzzes comfortably
like the promise that all is safe still

Mia Ayumi Malhotra

Mia Ayumi Malhotra is a fourth-generation Japanese American whose aesthetic inheritance includes the zuihitsu and fragmentary prose diaries of ancient Japan. In reclaiming this lineage, she resists powerful generational legacies of silence and assimilation, the result of mass incarceration during WWII. Through formal poetic innovation, she seeks to restore that which was torn, as in the practice of sashiko mending, in which ruined segments of fabric are artfully patched with decorative stitching. Her debut collection *Isako Isako* was a finalist for the California Book Award and the winner of the Alice James Award, the Nautilus Gold Award, a National Indie Excellence Award, and a Maine Literary Award. She holds creative writing degrees from Stanford University and the University of Washington, and her poems have appeared in numerous journals and anthologies, including *The Yale Review, Indiana Review,* and *Ink Knows No Borders: Poems of the Immigrant and Refugee Experience.*

Notes from the Birth Year: On Worlds That Leave Us

How easy to lift the baby into her crib, to hand her a cup. To watch
    her pull long sips of milk—*cow's* milk—from the spout.

Watching her, I am only faintly aware of the ritual that once
    sequestered us in a world of our own making: suckling,
    sustenance, skin.

The slow drift from wakefulness to sleep.

Now that she is weaned, how easy to live around the edges of that
    world. As though it never existed.

Though of course it did—and still does. Its shadows emerge in
      bedtime hush.

As in the moments after childbirth, when I felt very cold and
      strangely alone in my body. When, for the first time
      in her lifetime I carried not two heartbeats, but one.

How worlds create then leave us.

I am thinking of the nursery in Richmond my family once owned,
      roses run wild in their glass greenhouses.

The touch of Oxford in my in-laws' English.

The weary boulevards of Vientiane. The streets of Paris.

How world-haunted we all are.

The baby, now a toddler, bath-damp hair against my cheek—ode or
      elegy? Or both? For what is an ode without longing?

The absorption of two bodies, sealed in a single, fluid form.

The worlds that await—and those that never leave, whose ghostly
      edges we trace, wedged in the space

they leave us, gasping for breath.

Toward an Unfinished Work III (from "Daughters of Sarkhan")

> *I am detailing—which is to say: scouring/burnishing—*
> *the world I grew up in.*
> —Bhanu Kapil

How to write this world—its tangled jungles, mangrove roots. Its
      dengues and malarial fevers. A lost place. A departed place.

Memory is a series of light touches. If you touch something
      repeatedly it may come back to life. A burnished sheen.

During monsoon season, even the coconut fronds weep. Afterward,
      the city is stricken like a scorched throat—red dust everywhere.

You can write this world from the outside: its jungles. Or you can
      write it from the inside: fish sauce and oil spattered over open
      flame. Eels writhing on the dirt floor of the marketplace.

Or even deeper, within night's sweaty fist: the buzz of termites'
      jeweled wings. Drunken cicada drone.

Not all memory comes to light when touched. You can stroke a surface
      repeatedly—the flat surface of a river, for instance, but the only
      thing that will rise is a handful of bubbles.

This is not the sea we're talking about, but Mother River. Her droughts
      and fickle spells.

Touch the river. Touch it again—perhaps it will part, perhaps not.

Sheltering: Family Notebook

for my daughters, with lines from Louise Glück

Ready or not, here we are. We've been lost and found,
gone underground. We've raised cardboard cities,
pounded flowers to pulp. Danced like seeds, sprouting.
We've been Stuck in the Mud. We've pickled green beans
and carrots, watched spices rise to yeasty, bubbling surface.
We've traced ourselves in chalk, turned our bodies
to brilliant dust. We've learned to feast in the desert,
to braid bread, live bottled in, peppercorns and all.
We've shuffled in grocery lines and paged through
The New Yorker's grim spreads: emergency hospitals,
corpses stacked three deep. Around us, the death
toll rises. *Something comes into the world unwelcome
calling disorder, disorder—* Ordered home, we're baking.
It's Friday, and my daughters peer into the oven.
They miss school. They miss their friends. *I don't know
how much longer*, I say. Lost, too, in this interminable landscape.
Somewhere in the desert, my great-grandfather lifts
a stone from a dry creek bed. *Sui* meaning water,
seki meaning stone—*suiseki* as in *viewing stones*, naturally
formed. He brushes dirt from the rock's surface, sets it
on end. For days, he contemplates its dimensions.
A desolate island, perhaps—blueprint of some past
or future grief. So often, we've made life from dust.
First strawberries, then carnations. Roses, by trial
and error. Unearthed, we've found the white of bones,
wet of saliva, sound of singing—*at the end of my suffering
there was a door*. One day, we will reenter the house
of the living. A local party store texts: OPEN NOW!
FACE MASKS AND GLOVES FOR SALE!
My daughter chants rhymes, writes her name
for the first time. She's learning the names of things.
Virus. Yeast. Pandemic. She calls it the *pandemonium*.

Enculturation, they say, bringing a child into language—
from raw to cooked, from pale and unformed
to browned. Friday, she kneads dough. Monday,
she pushes stones into place, forms the letter "Y."
We touch the rough, chiseled edges and count
the days. Outside, fever rages. It's spring. She picks
flowers with her sister, wild irises with gold veins,
bellflowers with red and yellow striations. Their bodies—
so beloved, I sometimes mistake one for the other—
climb into bed beside me. The hours stretch, elastic.
Dusk lengthens over the trees. From my window,
I can see the neighbors' lit A-frame. I was once afraid—
I still am, but every night the sun sets, and in the gloaming,
a star—or is it the light from a plane—blinks on—

Meher Manda

Meher Manda is a poet, short story writer, culture critic, and educator originally from Mumbai, India, currently based in Brooklyn, New York. She earned her MFA in fiction from the College of New Rochelle where she was the founding editor-in-chief of *The Canopy Review*. She is the author of the chapbook *Busted Models* (No, Dear, 2019). Her fiction and poetry have been published in *Hobart Pulp, Epiphany Magazine, Los Angeles Review*, and elsewhere. She curates and co-hosts *An Angry Reading Series* in Harlem, New York, and writes for the political web-comic *Jamun Ka Ped*. Her poetry reaches out to multiple tongues from within the confines of the English language to extrapolate the stories of South Asian women.

Sisters on Gravel

in all the games, we played secret roles you wouldn't want to be
caught dead in, dangerous, swashbuckling butter knife-flingers,
with our mothers in the kitchen, we took mythical old-timey
       folktales,
twisted them in over our heads, we swung genders, played heroes,
tucked our skirts between our legs, we disrobed, took showers,
and cut through water with leaps and punts like wushu champions,
landing clumsily on naked butts, with our mothers in the kitchen,
we mixed soap and glycerin, and blew rainbow bubbles down to
wishing wells, watched them fly deep down below, slinging rocks to
measure the danger, daring and rescuing the sine qua non of our
       existence,
our mothers in the kitchen, we touched gently our plucky teats,
       compared notes
by squeezing tightly between our fingertips each body, we learnt to
       hold
by holding the other, we discovered textures, patterns, curves and
       edges

by walking over our bodies, noting down the twists and turns, our
        mothers
in the kitchen, we took kitchen playware, filled model vessels
        with dirt,
we collected rocks, crop shellings, plant offals, cooked meals for
        devils,
we refused to play woman, wrote stories with snakes in them, the
        snakes
were our friends, our mothers in the kitchen deep-fried cornballs to
        tame
our energies, imagined us as mothers in training while we yanked
        heads
off doll necks, we gave puppets crazy eyes, laughing witches-like, we
cleaved down plants from strange trees, rubbed their chunks on our
        shins
for magic, we played rough, we kissed roughly, we had to unlearn our
        kisses
to kiss others because we kissed each other ferociously, by choking
        pores,
we sucked the planet's air between our mouths, and poured it into each
        other,
our mothers in the kitchen, we loved with our bodies, our lips, we
        distilled
our love in secret homes, far into neglected backyards, my sister and
        I grew
to be unwomanlike together, to be everything our mothers in the
        kitchen were
not, so when my sister dropped my hand, she taught me my first
        lesson of
betrayal, when she sieved my name through love notes for a man,
        our mothers
stepped out of the kitchen to let me know—to be wild is to be
        temporary.

A Note from Indian Girls Who Hate Getting Naked

Somewhere in my past is an inadequate girl,
a half-formed person, her skin coagulated
like woven fabric, its marks stitched to reveal designs
of a local motif, stick-figured men riding horses along
parched river trails, a crumpled battlefield her body.
Day of full bloom with gulmohar leaves in syndicated repetition,
they put on the costume—an elongated stole going around
the breadth of her body, muscle cowering underneath.
This is the grand theme of our lives, masked and out of sight.

It isn't that they never taught us to love our bodies.
But that they never taught us to learn it.

This endless and perverse jig, of covering and un-showing,
limb and hide, fat and muscle, but never taught to pause,
to stare deeply and etch along stretch marks the sketch
that causes this brown shade to shine earthlike in moonlight.

Sorry for young girls who let slip gasps
when their *dupattas* reach for the ground.

Sorry for the women who created legends
by walking into funeral pyres, to defend honour
of body but not scalding skin.

Sorry for tying in honour to the body at all.

This raw plant, its petals curling into itself
pixels streaming in the rainbow of sunlight
what a joy its show of light. Its shameless display.

Sorry for cloaking it over, shamefully choking
its breathing pores, letting it desiccate underneath.
Wrapped like a ball of yarn cupped in the palm of a young boy
eager to please his fathers

who ask us why we're burning? Dissolving into fabric.
It is because our bodies are sweatshops. Our breaths rise above
like acrid smoke from chimneys, our systems churning productions.
We've not the pluck to unscrew our bolts, air out our rooms
and hang our nakedness to drip.

Aurora Masum-Javed

Aurora Masum-Javed is a Bangladeshi American poet and educator working on her first collection. A former Philip Roth Resident in Creative Writing and Hub City Writers House Resident, she received her MFA at Cornell, and has been a fellow at the MacDowell Colony, Millay Colony, Squaw Valley Community of Writers, Kundiman, Caldera Arts, Callaloo Creative Writing Workshop, and elsewhere. She believes the poem is a site of transformation, a space to investigate what is buried beneath all we cannot name. How do we find language for what's forgotten everywhere except the body—history's echoes storming through our cells? How do we unravel the architecture of the self? The family? The nation? As a writer, Aurora aims to exile nothing, to instead hold all of it, to unsuture the wounds and let them breathe.

Fine Lines

The barber traces the tall man's beard for the third time—
trim between the eyebrows, smooth fade of high top—
meticulous. I have always wanted this. Quiet love of men.
So I sit on the cracked leather couch, watch. A small boy
spins in his red chair, cape billowing like a gown. His father
cups a Corona beside me, hollers with every basket. Warriors
crush the Heat on three screens. Banter rises, breathes.
The boy eyes the blade near his face. Big Man, the barber
says, I got you. But I know his fear. The danger of a hand.
How in sixth grade Tony taught us to be boys. Fight, he said.
So we did. Raised fists, stiff, until our need was too big—
need to be anything but girls. How I hunted her then,
slammed her into brick, blood oozing from the back of her
head. Tony had never seen hurt like that. But I had.
My mother's. Abba with a bat in his fist. The footfall.
The crash. His body, cuffed, thrust to a bed of sirens.

The beginning of our end. Somewhere now, he slices a loaf
of bread, cradles the warmth of his second wife's breast.
Somewhere, he is gentle. He stays. And I am grown. Part
him. I've learned to sweeten men with my mouth. But here,
the barber's touch is just touch. Here, the boy twirls. Curry
fires a three. Every voice becomes a trumpet. Unabashed.
When the barber calls my name, I ask him to cut lines into
my head. I got you, he says. My lashes brush his wrist.
His hand lifts my chin.

After three cups of kava, I name every good thing
I never asked for:

like Liz washing dishes, the sexy deep
of the radio, that wet rag
she calls a sponge & me
pretending to read but really
just watching, sinking
like beach sand, both of us
stupid beautiful
in our sweatpants
& all I can think is
lucky lucky lucky
& once I begin, how can I stop:
Georgia the rescued rolling curlicue
into my belly, her fur
a furnace & years before:
that first boy, his fingers electric
inside me & further:
to when I climbed
every oak, spread my sweat-
drunk arms like a hero, free
fall of memory, down:

into the watercolor smooth
of mangoes, wilted box
at the bottom of the fridge,
I am thirteen & the Phantom
of the Opera croons from the busted
speakers, the ones older than I am & Amma
is singing, so I don't have to
say I'm sorry, just match her
off-key, we know all the words, or at least
we think we do & for the first time
in days, we're not yelling, she's
frying Rice Krispies, our American
muri, dancing the spatula above her head
& I'm on mango duty, finding
the mushiest ones, their brown sweet
blooming, Amma won't let me
cut them my way, the lazy way,
halved & checkered,
fold out, pop up candy, *No*,
she takes them & peels
the rinds slowly, they fall
spiraling & I pick up the skins, use my teeth,
suckle the meat, save the pit
for her because she knows how
to get at the marrow of a thing
better than I
ever could & for a moment, I see her
& how long it's been
since I looked,
      we sing & sing & she stomps
her slippered feet & I keep mine stuck,
bare, make beats with my hips,
we've always danced differently
& once we've eaten all
the throwaway things, we go in

for the slippery cubes, sugar-
drenched & bleeding
yellow & this is my favorite part
of morning, being with her,
eating with our naked hands,
our chins, cradles
for every good thing
leaking.

Lani T. Montreal

Lani T. Montreal is a Filipinx educator, writer, performer, and community activist based in Chicago. Her poems have been featured in journals and anthologies (among them, *Rattle, Bloodstone, Love Gathers All, Pinoy Poetics, Hay(Na)Ku 15,* and *MiPoesias*). In Fall 2018, Finishing Line Press published *FANBOYS: Poems about Teaching and Learning,* her first poetry collection. Lani writes poetry to create her home in the diaspora. She is the recipient of the 2015 3Arts Djerassi Residency and the 2008 3Arts Ragdale Residency. She is also a 2017 alumna of the Voices of Our Nation Arts (VONA) Writers' Workshop and a 2018 alumna of the Poetry Foundation Summer Teachers Institute. A former journalist in the Philippines, Montreal currently teaches writing at Malcolm X College, one of the City Colleges of Chicago, and writes a blog called "Fil-in-the-gap" (filinthegap.com). She lives and loves in Albany Park with her multi-racial, multi-species family.

Things to Remember from This Trip Back Home

You never bring enough clothes to the beach
It matters to look nice even in this heat, where
You sweat, stink, take more showers, sweat
Here, flavors explode without apology
Coffee is strong when brewed, but not when 3-in-1
Dessert is too sweet, too plenty
Don't be scared that someone in your family will go into a diabetic
     shock
Their blood is a quarter sugar
Your teeth will crumble into salt after eating something savory
You'll keep tasting *patis* long after you've left

Don't forget that here, people love hard
They are always teenagers in search of a high

Love is best when illicit
Lechon, when *de leche*
The sun sears your skin till it's crispy
The rains will give you *pulmunya*
Mosquitoes will fuck you over
As if you did them wrong in a previous life
They'll make your nose bleed; your blood platelet count, low

You will blow through your money like rain falling though broken roof
It is cheap, so cheap, you can get three massages in a week
Treat everybody to a movie
Buy things you will never use
Pasalubongs for people who didn't even know you left
Lives too are cheap, so cheap
People are shot for smoking weed; children, from sniffing glue
Ah, just collateral damage

Politicians have billboards the size of a building
No choice but to stare at them when stuck in traffic
And at whitening products peddled by *mestizas*

You will be stuck in traffic, more than once; in fact, more often than
          not
So don't forget to be patient, or maybe rent a personal hotspot, make
          sure
You're never without WiFi; always connected

Some days, though, the road is clear, not congested
Time matters, is not wasted waiting or looking at billboards
Or at crowds of passengers stranded at bus stops,
Waiting for a ride home past midnight

Remember, remember, because the gap steals your memory
You don't recall the bumpy ride on the jeepney at 2AM
How the men molested you with their sleepy heads

Their open legs
Their restless arms
Elbows that creep against your exposed skin

Don't forget you left your summer clothes behind,
Languishing in your sister's closet 'til your next visit
Your mother won't be giving them away to disaster victims

She's not there anymore.

Don't be wondering when summer in Chicago comes
And you can't find your blue dress
Remember you live in the in-between
Nothing is ever really lost.

Su Fang Ng

Born and raised in Malaysia, Su Fang Ng is ethnically Chinese and thoroughly Southeast Asian. Coming to the United States for college, she eventually earned a PhD in English from the University of Michigan, Ann Arbor, and is presently a professor of literature at Virginia Tech. Through poetry, she is exploring themes also important to her scholarship, the in-between spaces of identity and belonging, through and across languages.

Look at Her Mouth
(Lú khòaⁿ i ê chhuì)

Lú khòaⁿ i ê chhuì, lú khòaⁿ.
Look at her mouth, my father says,
Look at her mouth all twisted up.
My mother examines my face.
They agree my mouth is crooked
From speaking in the *ang moh*'s tongue.
My too excited retelling
Of my very first college year
In America cut short.
No one wants to hear me jabber,
Chatter 'bout my 'merican year:
Did I think I was holding court?

Lú khòaⁿ i ê chhuì, lú khòaⁿ.
Look at her mouth, my father says,
So *ang moh*, it's bent out of shape.
How can anyone understand
When she speaks with such strange accents,
And what has happened to her mouth?
Sharing father's fearful disgust,

123

Silenced, I examine my face.
The mirror shows a right-side tilt
In the curve of my lips and mouth,
While the left side seems to turn south:
Can there still be a saving grace?

Lú khòaⁿ i ê chhùi, lú khòaⁿ.
Look at her mouth, my father says,
It's all to do with Amer'ica,
Knew we should not have let her go.
Now she speaks in *ang moh* fashion
Who wants an alien in one's house?
Ashamed, I press my lips closed tight,
Acutely conscious how I speak,
Studying the mirror to make sure
To keep my mouth in a straight line,
As though crookedness were a sign
Of the linguistically impure.

Lú khòaⁿ i ê chhùi, lú khòaⁿ.
Look at her mouth, I remember
My father asking my mother,
Why is her mouth all twisted up?
Then I noticed in the mirror
My right eye smaller than my left,
My face's right side a trifle short,
Lips turned up a bit to one side.
And when I look across the room
I see the same *Hokkein* features
Just a tiny bit off-kilter,
Looking back with paternal pride.

Diana Khoi Nguyen

A Vietnamese American poet and multimedia artist, Diana Khoi Nguyen is the author of *Ghost Of* (Omnidawn, 2018), which received the distinctions of the 2019 Kate Tufts Discovery Award and Colorado Book Award; she was also a finalist for the National Book Award and *L.A. Times* Book Prize. Currently, Nguyen is an Assistant Professor at the University of Pittsburgh and also teaches in the Randolph College MFA. Of her poetics, she writes, "When we talk about the expanding universe, we mean that it has been growing since its beginning. The Big Bang. February 22, 2016: a new physics model predicts the universe had no beginning. With no origin story, there exists no status quo. I have no records of nothing. What I see, I do not yet know exists."

A Story about Holes

1.

A girl dug a hole at the beach, sent her siblings to fetch water.

I think she found pleasure in it. All things fall down, or want to,
so she dug and dug, her trowel falling deeper, the earth growing
        darker.

I think she thought in concentric circles, the tides coming
and going, overlapping each other. When she poured water in,
the hole filled up, then emptied, its walls caved in. She began again.
If she could have, she would have dug a hole every day, one
beside the other, then another, and another. A hole is a hole,
but none of them are the same.

Along a shore, no one can know how many holes there are.

Along a shore, no one can know which holes are hers.

2.

I typed my brother into a box. The search took 0.39 seconds and
there were as many entries as there were members of our family:
five, to be precise, four if you count the one who didn't think
he was one of us.

From Latin *praecis-* 'cut short', from the verb *praecidere,*
from *prae* 'in advance' + *caedere* 'to cut'.

There is a hole inside the search box. A hole
and a frame, to delineate where things go in. The internet
doesn't know my brother died. Oliver Nguyen at MyLife.com®
Age: 27.

He cut his one-year-old self out of each frame. Three, five,
shy of two, thirteen-year-old selves, too. Then at 24,
out of the whole picture.

Late in the evenings I walk in the middle of a road looking
forward, looking back, to see anything instead than nothing.

After death, does time keep on? Is he three now, or is it four?
I forget what day it is. About his birthday. Happy Afterlife,
no one says.

The road is empty. I go back to the box. "Oliver Khoi Nguyen . . .
no plus ones, no shares. Looks like you've reached the end. Looks
like you've reached the end."

3.

Hard to say, what could have happened.

—What happened?
—Happened?
—Yes.
—I didn't die.

All night the trees stand in lamplight. From out in the universe,
they are gliding about an axis. Staying still is a kind of moving.

Inside the still Ponderosa pines, silk-thin threads of water
sometimes break, exploding in small pops of music. A hole
in the air of their capillaries. A song of holes.

4.

I am a particle of the anti-past. A particle and its counterpart
quickly destroy each other. They blip into existence and then
they're out. The past and the anti-past multiply. 1 + 1 is 3.

As long as there are more particles than counterparts.

A history of particles: Once there were two particles, one
was a hole, the other had a stick. What came first, the hole
or the stick? I don't know, but soon there were more holes,
more sticks. Sticks found in holes, holes made by sticks.

Hawking showed that black holes can, like other holes, or sticks,
shrink and die. But there's a way out. Out of the black hole.

"If you feel you are in a black hole, don't give up—"

5.

This is a story about two particles. They are traveling near
an event horizon. Life at the edge can be peculiar. One
of the pair falls in, and the one who falls has a negative energy
which sucks out energy from the black hole.

The other particle, its counterpart, escapes with positive energy.
Naturally. No one knows why.

All night the pair stay silent in the dark, not touching.
The one who escapes informs us about the one who didn't.

This is a passing of their story from inside the black hole
to the outside. We used to think nothing ever came back out.

So here we are. One is here, the other one, over there, but
we know what happened to him. That he exists.

Alyssa Ogi

Alyssa Ogi is a Japanese and Chinese American writer from southern California. She received her MFA from the University of Oregon and edits books for Tin House in Portland, Oregon. An Elizabeth George Foundation grant recipient, she is at work on her first poetry collection, which re-imagines the histories and present-day complexities of the American West Coast. Her poems can be found in *Best New Poets*, *Poetry Northwest*, *Crab Orchard Review*, and elsewhere.

Tree Haibun

A mentor says my poetry is too preoccupied with race. There is nothing timeless about sensationalism, and he quotes Coleridge as if Coleridge parroted the words of God. He tells me to examine pine trees for wisdom. In this system, I am expected to be the best, expected to be obedient enough to excel, and I do. At everything, at once, not only on paper, but in the stall of a library toilet, where I throw up the words I've swallowed down all day. The burn feels natural, as if my great-great-grandmothers taught me how to purge in a dream. No one said that it'd feel cathartic; that the damage might be intentional. I'm preoccupied with my skin color in the light, and the weight of excellence around my belly. So yes, profess admiration that I can be the opposite of dangerous and the opposite of safe at once. Profess that a man snuck a hand up a modest skirt hem on a Los Angeles bus and I couldn't stop him, crushed by other passengers. I don't know what he looked like, though his cologne smelled like pine trees. I don't know why a man stopped my lover and me once, as we exited the Chandler Pavilion in our nicest clothes. Salieri's *The Great Kubla Khan of the Tartars* premiered; actors taped back their eyelids.

We left early to catch our bed. The strange man had
dimples like mine and asked where he could buy a girl like
me in the city. No one knew where his question was
directed: at a blond-haired American, at a black-haired
American, at a preoccupied laugh track long since
discarded. Two men laughed and one woman draped a
sweater over her obedient dress, with beadwork that
resembled trees across its hem. On the walk toward our
metro line, love reached for me. Love told me that some
people liked to get a rise out of others. I named the insult
sensational, but it came out as *timeless*. Love reached for me
and said I was overreacting, so I did what I do best.

Pine bends in snowstorms
until it breaks in the summer,
ill-prepared for warmth.

It's Rare That I Go Back to Unnamed Things

My kingdom, my cat, my country, my everything;
my hope for home is entirely free—
but I'm made to pay in inches and anxiety
and why did we think we could marry each other?

I happened to see the heart of a dog once,
roadkill to some, but an altar in the woods.
Someone draped it with a Confederate flag,
and I couldn't leave it there; they draped it
in second death, and I couldn't leave it there.
Maybe it had a name once (I wish I knew
how to bury it with a headstone for somebody's
mother). The water here is clearest in August,
I was told once; the dog is clearest at night

when I can't sleep. This morning I woke up
to two cats fighting, their screams like
children's screams, like countries, like an altar.

Love gave me a home in his clothes
and his mornings, and when I wear his shirt,
my breasts brag their ownership. The kingdom,
my castle, my nothing I couldn't see; the dog
like a child, like our child who haunts me.
A flag, an altar, I want to brag of motherhood,
but that was left in the woods where no one
could find it. Ten weeks, and I'm close to you,
ten weeks; you're still gone from me.
For a second, I forget the home I have buried
as I've tried to forget everything new.
The woods, my nameless, a heart for roadkill,
why must I be the one to remember you?

Cynthia Dewi Oka

Cynthia Dewi Oka is the author of three books of poems: *Fire Is Not a Country: Poems* (Northwestern University Press, 2021), *Salvage: Poems* (2017) and *Nomad of Salt and Hard Water* (Thread Makes Blanket, 2016). She has been awarded the Leeway Foundation's Transformation Award and the Amy Clampitt Residency. In 2017, she created Sanctuary: A Migrant Poetry Workshop for immigrant poets based in Philadelphia. A graduate of the MFA Program for Writers at Warren Wilson College, she is originally from Bali, Indonesia, and currently teaches creative writing at Bryn Mawr College. For her, poetry is the practice of freedom.

Conditions of Peace

1. Still, the cities smile. When I say buckle, I mean two exiles
whose origin is love; one to excise nightmare from the flesh
by embedding night in the flesh, red hands not hesitating those
long afternoons when sheets heavy with ash puffed their cheeks
in the yard where light lay bleating while stray cats in the roof
curled bonelessly around their disfigurements like shells in
the wrack line. The other a capacity the body, pressed, a slow-
leaking berry in the glass jaws of capital, has already forgotten.

2. Night with the force of religion: nothing was told, nothing was
hidden. The dictator understood more than the poet or prophet
the life of dew on orchids that smeared themselves shamelessly
on days of volcanic dust. Amaranth, midnight, plum. More than
enough to fret about. The aunt for whom confession meant spying
on the orphaned maid with the new priest-in-training. The uncle
who swore his Marlboro sticks were packed with grass. Man-size
bags of feathers in case the neighbors tried to burn us down again.

3. Sometimes when I am not speaking with my mother, because
the night survives in my flesh in unintended ways, which in turn
causes her pain, I think of her angular in hospital whites, the flies
like scrambled letters in bulbs dying over her head as she bowed
to hear the last requests of syphilitics whose last blisters were
exploding like the nation's censored histories. Men too guilty
to marry or made guilty by marriage whose solace now was her
silence, which like nothing else they'd ever seen, did not waver.

4. This is not memory, but something I should have remembered:
a dark figure sweeping roach husks from under the table at sunrise.
It paused as it lifted the pan over the short wall that separated yard
from dining hall – the dead insects were too smooth, their blackness
shared too much of the flatness of just-after-dusk. A closer look
(in the gap between the wall and the underside of clay tiles, smoke
forearms punching in slow motion the red-ribbed sky) revealed
an absence of eyes, wings, legs. Only paint, and threads of keratin.

5. A manicure takes about thirty minutes. In that time, I allow
myself not to wonder about the distances between my desk and
the salon, my desk and my mind, the salon and balconies of paddy
ripening, paddy and the scythe, paddy and the village, paddy and
the concept of green, green and camouflage, green and the agent
called Orange, agent and wire and the collapse of the epiglottis,
collapse and the faces on the boat, faces that repeat with slight
alterations, faces that do not and my mind, slightness and beauty

6. in the sense of irretrievable behind the surgical mask and this
woman who makes hands beautiful to put her son through college,
her son and my son, my son and language I cannot give, language
that scythes, that paddies, that greens even the forearms of hell,
hell and what this woman is not afraid of, hell and a pair of human
hands, hands and wax and specters on the wall that war and dance,
war and dance, war and acetone and ultraviolet light, light and faces
that do not alter. Do not and God. Every God is a god of distance.

7. I go to the sea to drown. Not to die among the daily bodies,
their worries etched on by shrieking children and gulls. This is a
       kind
of silence. Sometimes I walk up and down the stairs in my house
a few times before bed to make sure the doors are locked. I see that
they are. I remember seeing and touching them moments ago. But each
time, I take the bolts in my hand and turn, just to feel them fail to turn
any further. I beat my son once because he stole. A mother, buckling,
keeps things in their places. *This* grassless history. *That* surviving
       night.

Ami Patel

Ami Patel is a queer, diasporic South Asian poet. She was born in San Jose, California, and moved around the East Coast before her family settled in Corona, California, where she grew up in a boisterous Gujarati community. Ami's writing blossomed in APIA poetry and spoken word communities. She is a two-time VONA fellow, a 2010 Visual Communications Armed with a Camera Fellow, and featured her theatrical work in East West Players' Evoke: South Asian Voices Festival in 2013. Her most recent written work can be found in *Unchaste Anthology*, Volume Two and Issue #2 of the *Madwoman Etc.* zine.

faltering, and yet

My parents call me chakli—little bird—their firstborn
flitting through the channel of my mother, emerging
as shiny forehead and warring gaze. I arrive in late spring
but that first winter comes too soon, the three of us
frigid and unfamiliar with Philly, far from grandparents
and great-grandparents and stores full of spices
with names I still only know in Gujarati. I don't sleep.
I shriek and spittle, I confound, a sharp avian thing
speaking in tongues. My father returns home later and later,
his eyes closing on the couch before 9 p.m. dinners and me
sprawled on him, both bodies syncing to the tunes of tired.
My mother is overwhelmed, more so than she lets on.
The fridge hums incessantly, the halogen sallows our faces.
The small TV stays on during feedings, naptimes, diaper changes.
While she cooks, grainy brown bodies shimmy across the screen.
My first memories are of beehive hairdos and benevolent mustaches,
of the croons of Lata & Asha echoing through the lonely.
Months go by. My first moves emerge thunderously

with the conviction of a boxer. My father tells me decades later
he was afraid to hold me. His fears fused together like hot metal
and gilded them to the smallest vessel in his eyeline, to me,
the one bearing his name. The one still trying to crack through
those same fears, of body, of being, still learning how to fly,
sore and tumbled by the feat of it all.

Yamini Pathak

Yamini Pathak is a former software engineer, born and raised in India. Her poetry and non-fiction have appeared in *Waxwing, Anomaly, The Kenyon Review* blog, *The Hindu* newspaper, and elsewhere. Her chapbook, *Atlas of Lost Places*, is published by Milk and Cake Press. A Dodge Foundation Poet in the Schools, she is the poetry editor for *Inch* (Bull City Press) and an MFA candidate at Antioch University, Los Angeles. Yamini is an alumnus of VONA/Voices (Voices of Our Nations Arts Foundation), and Community of Writers. She lives in New Jersey with her husband and two sons.

पकड़ Pakad

Hindi.

noun. signature musical phrase, identifies a raaga in North Indian Classical music.

verb. hold, catch, capture, cling, preserve, protect.

We were taught our languages were crude.
Imagine a ghazal   the verses threaded into a
       labyrinth   each couplet a shifting
              tunnel that leads to
the winking jewel   at its heart.
Witness a mushaira in the dim
              lanes of Ghalib's Delhi,
the passing   of the lamp in a circlet of poets   as each
recites   the interjections of   *wah!wah!*   all that is
capsuled in the pearl of a single syllable.

We were convinced our table manners were savage.
We sat criss-crossed anyhow   on the floor,
families loud, children opening
              their mouths to a loving

invasion   rice grains pinched in the beaks
of their mothers' fingers
            The trickle of juices warming the purse
of our palms before they entered
the realms of our tongues.

We grew to despise our sun-blissed skins.
We believed fair   was lovely   applied
unguents designed to exhibit
our lovely, plastic selves to the world
Our Gods remain
                        toned by dusk
Shyam   divine
flute between lips   jaunty
peacock feather tucked in his curls
Nataraja, arms akimbo, feet drumming in cosmic
ballet   face and chest smeared in ash
Kali   tender & terrible   color of your
worst nightmares
Our pre-dawn raagas   still dark-threaded   still
throb with the sweet
      wet of morning mist.

Ahimsa

It is not enough/ To love you. It is not enough to want you destroyed.
  - Terrance Hayes

If someone loved me   then cut the birds from my tongue
expeller-pressed the air from my lungs   one wing at a time
dismembered me   could I look back with the
lotus eyes of compassion   see how they stain themselves?
gouge and bleed?   Could I join them in the darkroom
dip negatives   in a chemical bath   peg the damp

curls of nascent photographs from our lives
                              on a clothesline to drip dry overnight?
Would you judge me a fool if I said my love
is a parched well that never quits reaching for the aquifer?
Born under a water-sign, I fight different   Canyons are hewn
by a licking stream   a tongue worrying stone after stone
like loosened teeth   My love-song is a blood-song   survival-song

The bird boxed by night sings for us both

Kailee Pedersen

Kailee Pedersen was adopted from Nanning in 1996 and is of Chinese Dai descent. She grew up in Nebraska, where her family owns a farm. Her poetic work blends her adoptee background with mythology and is further influenced by her BA in Classics from Columbia University. She is the recipient of a 2015 Individual Artist Fellowship in Nonfiction from the Nebraska Arts Council, winner of the 2017 New South Prose Contest, and winner of Gival Press's Oscar Wilde Award for best LGBTQ poem. She is currently finishing a novel.

Kaguya-hime, or The Bamboo-Cutter's Daughter

I think my white father should have sliced
                                                         the bamboo higher.

                        I think he should have swung his sickle and
                                                cut me
                                                        in half.

Michelle Peñaloza

Michelle Peñaloza is the author of *Former Possessions of the Spanish Empire*, winner of the 2018 Hillary Gravendyk National Poetry Prize (Inlandia Books, 2019). She is also the author of two chapbooks, *landscape/heartbreak* (Two Sylvias, 2015), and *Last Night I Dreamt of Volcanoes* (Organic Weapon Arts, 2015). The proud daughter of Filipino immigrants, Michelle was born in the suburbs of Detroit, Michigan, and raised in Nashville, Tennessee. She now lives in rural Northern California on the land of the Round Valley Indian Tribes.

Post Diaspora

Elsewhere, butterflies mean something
I cannot remember—luck or life
or death or maybe it depends on
where the fluttering wings appear.
How exhausting (or dangerous)
to forget always what means what
where. How do you say *butterfly?*
Alitaptap? Tutubi? Or is that
dragonfly? Or *lighting bug?*
How do you say *I'm sorry* or *I miss you*
or *I don't know how not to forget?*

                    *

Today's wonder: a river that begins
straight up from the ground as if
from nowhere. The trees around it ask—
but, *where were you born?*
Ultimately, which means more?
The seed's first wink? Or the root's first tip-toe?

Parents speak of before: *when you were but*
a twinkle in your father's eye. What hope
is born from the dust of those stars.

*

There's a saying: those who do not swim
deep in the waters from which they came
cannot arrive in the oceans they hope to go.
My parents began an ocean away
and arrived in a land of lakes and snow.
I've been back to their water (is it mine, too?)
but, wasn't a good swimmer.
Everyone spoke underwater; I could only
hold my breath to listen for so long.
I did learn the water carries its own song.

*

The discipline of joy is about survival.
You make your own joy—
this is the work my mother taught me.
Little factory, little mine of reminders—
find, make, joy to sustain multiple life-
times: the blanket made beautiful
from patterned found scraps;
the broth of tap water and ginger and bones.
What fullness my mother earned
and could stuff inside an envelope
to send each month back home.

*

We all carry flags
whether we mean to

or not. I've grown more and more
suspicious of nation-
hood, the more and more I've had to
explain my face. I always had
a tough time with placing
my hand over my heart.
Holding it in my palm
was what my parents taught me.

*

My mother says: *You are a happy person.*
Write poems that show that.
I think she worries
my anger is a reflection
of where she went wrong.
I don't know how to
make her understand my anger
is a gift that she gave me.
Years of her gazing at the ground,
years of her prayer so that I could
decide to believe or not;
to use my mouth or keep it shut.

*

My mother proofreads my LinkedIn.
Are you stalking me on the internet,
Ma? I text an emoji after so she knows
I'm mostly kidding. She sends me a
prayer given to the children of Fatima
by the Virgin Mary. We text this way
when talking makes us sigh or cry
with what we don't know. Too much
unsaid pinches beneath everything

we utter—our *modus operandi*—
I love you: you disappoint me: I love
you: you expect too much: I love you:
I say aloud all the wrong
words: I love you.

*

There are debts we carry
inside our insides—
debts that live in the spleen,
the liver, the stomach, the heart.
I think I carry my debts
owed my mother
inside my teeth, which have been
bound and corrected and polished
and whitened, year after year.
My mother's mouth is full
of white teeth and pink gums
made in a lab, made many years
after the loss of her own born smile.

*

Absence is what took me
so long to name after many years
of scrying the world for answers:
Why does this hollow live
inside my aching throat?
When the anemone's kisses cling
to my fingertips, what does it mourn?
What is my mother's greatest fear
and my father's last legacy?

Angela Peñaredondo

Angela Peñaredondo is a queer Filipinx interdisciplinary writer, artist, and educator. Peñaredondo is author of the chapbook *Maroon* (Jamii Publications, 2015) and *All Things Lose Thousands of Times* (Inlandia Institute, 2016), winner of the Hillary Gravendyk Poetry Prize. Peñaredondo's work has appeared in The Academy of American Poets, *Black Warrior Review, Southern Humanities Review* and elsewhere. Peñaredondo is a Kundiman, VONA/Voices of our Nations Art fellow, Macondista as well as an Assistant Professor of Creative Writing and Digital Humanities at California State University San Bernardino.

Why Grandmother Became a Minke Whale

Underwater, she endures. Attempts to create a viable future in the shifty green among the other whores and feminists. Akin to the frilled sharks in cabaret and all that teeth. The wide paddle mouth of a pelican eel, the angler in their grotesque horniness harmonizes with her obsessions for hairy antennae oscillating in the dark.

Above, parties of war continue. On land, what's there to need? Mud, stools. The salacious heat.

Certainly, she has mended enough quilts and cotton to comfort her husband's sweat soaked body for nights and those late rough nights. No more rice or pickled singkamas or goat knuckle stew that she fed the soldiers in their heavy boots, using up all the spoons and her pretty effigies. They always say, with their mouths stuffed with porridge and belly meat, *you sure have some legs.*

Let her have ocean. Gargantuan, iridescent-cunt-kaleidescoping to the
     Black Sea.
Map. Clock. Contract. Kill. They all mean something different down here.

Oysters and mussels, she'll gulp them down with no desire for palm
wine. She'll read books floating on her side, the celestial of algae
tickling her brain and wanted curvy fat. In that unreachable sky some
human might describe as precious or turquoise, she knows paradise
lives elsewhere.

Megan Pinto

Megan Pinto is a poet of Indian descent. She grew up in Raleigh and now resides in Brooklyn, New York. Megan is currently at work on her first collection of poetry, which explores the Indian diaspora, faith, and visual art. Her poems can be found in *Ploughshares*, *Lit Hub*, *RHINO*, and elsewhere. She has received scholarships from Bread Loaf and the Port Townsend Writers' Conference, and an Amy Award from Poets & Writers. She holds an MFA in Poetry from Warren Wilson College.

After Odysseus

Here, in the clinic, a therapist
asks the child to draw a picture
of her body—to color all the places
where it hurts, and color all the places
where it feels good. No medical examiner,
no jury, just a child and her pencils—in this
version, she is taller than the trees. Outside,

it is winter, and slow cars make tracks
through the snow. I hold blank paper
with both hands as I imagine the cyclops held
his weeping eye. Around him: upturned dirt
and footprints. Did he focus on the scent
of the sea? Though still, it must have lingered
in the air—the scent of citrus and men. Alone,
he counted his slaughtered brothers, while dead
sheep roasted in the sun. I know what it is to stand

at the edge of someone else's story. The therapist
retreats to the hallway, but leaves

the door ajar. The child in this moment
is calm. She is playing a game with her hands:
She is catching every ray of light
through the window, late afternoon and brilliant.

To the Old Man Who Lived on a Hill

He was looking for news of the world. He was looking for his daughter
who died in the fire, the car that burst into flames, the crash,
his wife who left him for her lover. He was looking

at the world through a window in the den, where he kept the photographs
and the heater, the air conditioner and the dog treats, the trophies
from spelling bees and dance recitals. He was looking at how light

changed the texture of shadows, petals on the lawn. Spring
is ending here, and dust collects on rows of encyclopedias lining
the shelves, on the heavy crucifix hanging on the wall. It is morning,

it is night. The television flickers, muted: documentary, documentary,
pornography, documentary, the news. I was hired to give him a reason
to live, and to rid the kitchen of its spoiled food, to clean droppings

from the dogs, from the bird that got in through the basement,
to convince him to sleep in his bed, and not on the plastic lined
mattress in the guest room. His back ached. There is a sadness,

and then there is the thing beyond sadness. 4:00 a.m. infomercials,
roaches marching over the expanse of cracked walls, trying
to masturbate and finding you cannot, wanting your dogs

to love you, and knowing they will eat you when you die.
You could learn to change, you could learn to apologize,
you think, if given the chance. For a few hours of work

I collect $70 a day, talk about the weather, dogs, politics.
I take the rotting food and replace it with green things. I watch
his face animate, change, go blank for hours in the afternoon.

Then a thought slides down, like morning dew
on spider silk—it lingers for a moment, it tries to transform.

Preeti Kaur Rajpal

Preeti Kaur Rajpal is a Sikh poet. She grew up in California's San Joaquin Valley. Preeti first began writing as a student of June Jordan in her Poetry for the People program. Preeti's poems can be found in *The Lantern Review*, *Tupelo Quarterly*, *Jaggery Lit*, and other publications. She is a recent Jerome Hill Artist Fellow in Literature. Her first book of poems is forthcoming.

watching the wagah border closing ceremony

i watch peacocks strut
in turbans and khaki salute
soldiers kick legs into air
paper kites that neighbor children
fly cutting each other's wire
scissors in fire wheat sky
rifles click the countries' teacups
clacking cheer of border fence
i sit with the Indians
under august's only sun
instead of with the American
tourists in the v.i.p.-booth

view of circus tent locks
clear from paper map unrolled
steel wall electric with nuclear
blood running the great-grandmother's
wrist ash left on other side
grand trunk our hair's wheel
flags rising falling the breath
borders inherited the sugar
my family dead by 47
tumbling pigeons who cross god
gates pulled down at sunset
light scattering in half

Shazia Hafiz Ramji

Shazia Hafiz Ramji lives in Vancouver, British Columbia. She grew up in England and Kenya in a Muslim family of Indian, Pakistani, Persian, and Irish descent. Her first book, *Port of Being*, was written in the grip of an obsession with surveillance and ports, which grew after she was stalked. Ports, cities, and addiction are recurring themes in her poems, essays, and stories. More recently, Shazia has been inspired by themes of faith, family, and the meaning of home. She is at work on a novel.

Leopard Dream Symbol

Last night I dreamt of a leopard on the roof
of the convenience store down the road from my place.

I was inside a car at almost night-time when I saw its fur
gleam past the antennas, its spots hidden under a wet skin

as if it had swum in tar or a dead swamp. When I woke up,
I entered "Leopard Dream Symbol" into my phone. I was told

what I wanted to hear: that it was a good omen, even though
I maced its face when it jumped onto the car where I was sitting

next to my dad. It had seen us there. The Great Watcher
is also one of its names, because of its spots that are like eyes.

Because leopards are protective of their little ones, I am told
I have a craving to be protective towards my family.

That makes too much sense for a dream with a leopard in it.
Then again, in almost every dream I have of my family,

there's a big cat against me and I'm the only one who's seen it.
I'm the only one who can do something.

When I was little, my parents told me I was too stubborn, too
kind. They nicknamed me Azadi, the word spoken by

freedom fighters, meaning independence. My phone tells me
about adversity, that leopards overcome it, that I am more aware

of my surroundings if they appear in a dream. So I say hello
to this rare animal that appeared two days before the dream

in the place where I grew up, where I had first seen a sign of the
         big cat
on a sign that told me a man had died there after a leopard leapt off.

This is not what I want Leopard Dream Symbol to remind me of:
one of my homes, where this man was mauled by a leopard.

My parents are visiting this home and I'm surprised
by how terrified I am about bombs and dirty water,

about the currency exchange and big cats, about not being able
to be there for them. "I love you guys," I tell them. "Don't

walk alone at night!" My dad is surprised
I would say such a thing, being Azadi,

so they go their own way and feast on baobab and kebab,
they walk the beach as if they're on a second honeymoon.

"See you later," they say, "we'll bring some for you!" They are so
         stubborn
and so kind. They won't use Wi-Fi because they're drinking out of
         coconuts.

They're home for the first time in ten years. They remind me
that a leopard cannot change its spots.

Swati Rana

Swati Rana was born in India and also calls Canada and the United States home. Her work is based in the alluring yet often inscrutable landscapes around her, which speak a language she tries to capture: a record of human and interspecies dispossession, migration, violence, and resettlement. Her poems inhabit her biography while ranging small and large, from the quotidian to the epochal dimensions of diasporic life. Rana studied poetry at Dartmouth College and at University of California, Berkeley. Currently, she teaches in the English Department at University of California, Santa Barbara. Rana's work has appeared in *The Paris Review*, *Granta*, *Crazyhorse*, *The Asian American Literary Review*, *Wasafiri*, and *The Dalhousie Review*, as well as other publications.

Plane Ride after 9/11

Sash is half
down to block the sun
coming out instead

of its reflection
in the ocean.
Waves are still

moving minutely
like sand. A boat
blemishes hills

of water, more boldly
shaded by the drag
of clouds. Where ocean

ends and sky
begins, can't say,
a heavy ledge

then lighter grey
retreating. Clouds mount
the horizon, soundless,

aroused by a wide
mad expanse.
The coast intrudes,

casts an edge,
but the sun
is driving

up the mouth
of an estuary.
This is where we begin

to exist
upon the fetid
soil, its long

cultivated skin,
the effort
of order exerted

on a landscape.
A furious shine passes
over lakes, ponds,

metal siding.
The plane slants aside
till the earth's face

meets mine,
horizon climbs up
then down again through

clouds, cavernous
breath. Spit out,
we break from land

traces, abridged
sky. The hot cabin
is like waking

from a restless
night, window
closed too tight—

Suddenly
I see another plane
fly in the opposite

direction, occult
mirror of the sky
briefly revealed

to contain
our own precarious
situation. I see myself

peering
from below a half
downed sash,

brown skin,
a kind of
terror.

Karen Rigby

Karen Rigby is a Chinese/Panamanian/American poet born in the
Republic of Panama. She is the author of *Chinoiserie* (Ahsahta Press,
2012). A 2007 National Endowment for the Arts literature fellow, her
poems have been published in *The Spectacle, Australian Book Review,*
and other journals. She views poetry as a space for open-ended questioning, and is influenced by the visual arts, pop culture, and the 20th
century. She lives in Arizona.

After a Line by Montaigne

Because the Renaissance is a house whose rafters
are stenciled in Latin, and the ribs of a dolphin
lace with kelp, easy to build little romances,
little aches to hold the story in place:
how I loved him *because it was he,*
because it was I, trees cupping the sky
like Montaigne's room lit by firelight,
but truer to say I thought love would save me
from that teenage midland no one believes
will end—K-mart cutoffs and filigreed rings—
but it ends, 1992 far gone enough to be
the vanishing point erased after all other lines
are drawn. Isn't it better the story frayed
before the boy named for an apostle
turned a gun on that motherless wind?
A throat holds as much song as you let it.
The span between a bird's wings the same as a fist.

Sun Yung Shin

Sun Yung Shin is a Korean American poet, editor, and writer whose work has appeared in *POETRY, BOMB* magazine, the 2021 Gwangju Biennale, and elsewhere. Her poetry collections have won an Asian American Literary Award and a Minnesota Book Award. Her fourth book of poems, *The Wet Hex*, will be published by Coffee House Press in 2022. With poet Su Hwang she co-directs Poetry Asylum in Minneapolis.

Modal Verbs of a Korean Migration

> *"The public sphere is constituted in part by what cannot be said and what cannot be shown."*
>
> —Judith Butler, *Precarious Life: The Powers of Mourning and Violence*

1. It is necessarily true that being born under the public sphere of the Park Chung-hee dictatorship may cause a child to dream of dead wives and choir girls.
2. It was possible that attempted assassinations of one's former ruler in the public sphere would cause even more rapid industrialization of most labor.
3. The private sphere duty of a woman would be to carry dead children, inside or outside of her body.
4. An obligation could be fulfilled in the public sphere by the naturalized citizen as well as by a legal alien.
5. Death is not your last public obligation.
6. Being an auxiliary child is not the end of the private world.
7. The end of the public world shall make everyone auxiliary.
8. You had better choose your private possessions carefully because they might spell your name after death.
9. Continuity of the private self meets the public self at midnight, and there it can wash its many hands.
10. What cannot be shown and what cannot be said inside the labyrinth of mourning becomes public on the surface of the body, settling under the eyes, absorbing sunlight.

Raena Shirali

Raena Shirali is an Indian American poet, educator, and editor from Charleston, South Carolina. Shirali is the author of *GILT* (YesYes Books, 2017), which won the 2018 Milt Kessler Poetry Book Award. Winner of a Pushcart Prize and a former Philip Roth Resident at Bucknell University, she is also the recipient of prizes and honors from VIDA, *Gulf Coast, Boston Review, & Cosmonauts Avenue*. Shirali is an Assistant Professor of English at Holy Family University in Philadelphia, where she is also Co-Editor-in-Chief for *Muzzle Magazine*. Hers is a poetics of fragmentation and liminality; in recent work, she interrogates her positionality as privileged member of the American Empire in relationship to the ongoing practice of witch hunting in India. Shirali's work holds up a double-sided mirror between Western and Indian cultures' treatment of women, incorporating anthropological research and interviews with survivors into the poems themselves.

lucky inhabitant

failing to conjure even distant relatives i know not

which women precede me, believe all this pain is at least
our own   on my lap the books theorize

[witchcraft is no longer a personal matter]

state plainly [the women had nails
driven into their foreheads] & full up now with steel

& scythes & a list of weapons wielded

against us, am nauseous & taking it personally   though
at least am not asked to detail my assault on television

holding my chin up for photographers   dubbed *icon*

& simultaneously driven out of the nation
yes   you might say this makes me one of the lucky

inhabitants   yes   here there are no jackfruit

trees but in a chamber the semicircle of [men had red eyes—
the kind of eyes that saw no reason and were filled

with cruelty] & somewhere online i am blamed

for not remembering yes gone now my willful ascension
the stairs, his room & i don't fight back know what fate awaits

women who protest too much no matter dialect

or country the question is the same   *ki jani*   they ask
in the motherland   & *who knows*   here we throw up

our hands & it isn't in prayer

there's blood in the soil so they call it *filth*   blood
on our legs so they call us *gone*   they're not wrong

& they will not   be fooled, won't take   it back

it's night & the jackfruit trees close in   there's chanting
in the distance who owns   this world

self-portrait in the oppressor's vernacular

told pretty for a light-skinned black girl / you are what you eat / told
bitches gotta eat / & the fuck's an aloo / told 36-24-36 / modest's
hottest / told not quite a 6-out-of-10 / told rock it braless / told
tape those down / everyone can tell you're cold / & you dress
like a *terrorist* / told come on / just show us / told avoid
eye contact / told girl / you lookin' thick today / told cover
the back of your neck / oh my god you tan *sooo* quickly / told no
cover up in that shade / we can see your nipples / told sheer's
the new black / told you're the new black / told not-black
enough / told not-desi enough / told pretty as a white girl /
told upper caste / told female circumcision / told witches hunted
in the country you call *homeland* / told you're just lucky
to be here / told life begins at consummation / told only *sluts*
take birth control / stop acting so american / told ration's
king / told get an education / stop acting like a crazy / told *bitch*
/ but i don't think of you as indian / told get on your knees / told
bitch / your hips are for gripping & riding / told swallow / told always
swallow / told they think it's *sooo* hot all you have to do is swallow
& make eye contact but not for too long / told gold
makes brown skin glow / told silver's cheap & you a bad
bitch / told stop whining *pussy* by the cop who pushed you
against a palm tree / told just like the rest of these *immigrants* /
told entitled / told spoiled / told mop up the shit
in the coffee shop bathroom / you're fifteen &
the twenty-one-year-old line cook gives you a cigarette
every time you flash him / told *bitch* you gotta work
for that money / told only *sluts* work for their money / so pretty
you won't have to work a day in your life / told you only got
one life & look at you out here
wasting it.

C.E. Shue

C.E. Shue is a third generation Chinese American who grew up in a rural, non-Asian farming community in Southern California. A Kundiman Fellow, she writes poetry, fiction, and essays that reflect the kaleidoscopic nature of identity and how elements of race, gender, culture, and age recombine in one's life and art. Her work has been published in *Entropy*, *Drunken Boat*, *The 92nd Street Y* and *Washington Square Review*, and her story, "Every Now and Then," was a finalist in the Gold Line Chapbook Contest. The recipient of scholarships and grants from The University of San Francisco, The Provincetown Fine Arts Workshop, and The Vermont Studio Center, she has read at Litquake, The Kearny Street Workshop, and Quiet Lightning, among other venues. C.E. is currently working on a novel, *Assimilation Mountain*.

How to Bind a Book of Fortunes

1. Place seven fortune cookie fortunes together, each one nested inside the other.
   Be on the lookout for coming events; they cast their shadows beforehand.

2. Fold four equal-sized circles in half.
   Sometimes two small jumps are better than one big leap.

3. Draw an arrow on waxed paper.
   Joys are often the shadows cast by sorrows.

4. Rethread the needle with another color of thread.
   Results are the echoes of your actions.

5. Try to remember which way the grain of the paper is going.
   Let your heart make your decisions - it does not get as confused as your head.

6. Tie an overhand knot.
   How can you have a beautiful ending without making beautiful mistakes?

7. Type a random string of letters.
   Be patient: in time, even an egg will walk.

8. Turn your project inside out.

*Numbered lines are instructions collected from *Unique Handmade Books* by Alisa Golden (Sterling Publishing Company, Inc., New York, 2003). Italicized lines are sayings found in fortune cookies.

Monica Sok

Monica Sok is a Khmer poet and the daughter of refugees. She is the author of *A Nail the Evening Hangs On* (Copper Canyon Press, 2020). She has received fellowships from Hedgebrook, Kundiman, MacDowell, National Endowment for the Arts, and others. Sok is a Jones Lecturer at Stanford University and teaches poetry at the Center for Empowering Refugees and Immigrants in Oakland, California. Her poetry explores intergenerationality while mythologizing personal and collective histories. A major theme in her work is familial silence and inherited traumas, which she addresses through narratives grounded in resilience and empowerment.

ABC for Refugees

Cherub-bee-dee how does a man
who doesn't read English well know that cherub-bee-dum
those aren't really words-bee-dee.
But birds.

Cherub-bee-dum, he stumbles, reading to me
by the sliding glass door cherub-bee-dee, through which I watch
my brother play in the dum-dum-yard.

Cherub-bee-dee, Cherub-bee-dum, like how my father says
Fine then! Leave! My mother shouts, *Stupid! Dumb!*
We live in a small bee-dee-nest too, one hallway to bee-dum-slam
   doors.

Birds? What are birds?
Thanks to my father, reading with me, I have more feathers.

T-H-E. First word he ever taught me to pluck . . .
It is a word used all the time. Cherub-cherub-bee-dum!

The mail. The mailbox. The school bus. *The the.*

He asks me to read the mail. Not birds, *mail.*
If you don't read this, you will turn into birds.
And I read it to him the best I can.
The end. A feather. Two feathers. The. The end.

Mother, mother. Repeat after me.
Cherub-bee-dee, Cherub-bee-dum!
We read together before bedtime.

In a Room of One Thousand Buddhas

The water in my heart was falling. To my right
a row of Buddhas in meditation
sheltered by the Naga snake but this snake was real,
unlike the American and the heads in his cabinet.
The Naga protected the Buddha from rain,
spread its seven hoods to keep him dry.
And did I tell you it was raining all day?
I bought a poncho to ride around Siem Reap.
Rain during the dry season. Buddha calling on the Earth
for witness. Something water protectors
at Standing Rock are doing right now. Protecting water
because water is life. But a night of rubber bullets
and tear gas and water hoses, that is not life.
Today too, while eating breakfast noodles in my hotel
Neo-Nazis saluted back home in Harrisburg.
They were not calling on the Earth, their palms up
but facing down. Looking at the Buddha,

I thought he looks like me.
Some with broader shoulders, some from pre-Angkorian
and Angkorian times, some from this century,
four sitting back-to-back in a circle
each in different mudras. Sandstone. Wood. Stone.
Depending on what was available
or how kings chose to perpetuate who they worshipped.
Sitting on the coils of the Naga. Eyes closed.
Or looking down. Some looked scared. Calm.
Some with hands missing or cracked down the side.
Some looked starved. Their clothes shattered.
One, wooden, was defaced standing.
Except for a small curve of lip and one shut left eye.
There were others, smaller, small as people.

Celina Su

Celina Su was born in São Paulo, Brazil, to Chinese parents, and lives in Brooklyn, New York. She is the author of *Landia* (Belladonna* Press, 2018). Her writing includes the poetry chapbooks *Plurality Decree* (MIEL Books, 2015) and *Beyond Relief* (with Ariana Reines, Belladonna*, 2013), three books on the politics of social policy and civil society, and pieces in journals such as the *New York Times Magazine*, n+1, and *Harper's*. Su is the Marilyn J. Gittell Chair in Urban Studies and a Professor of Political Science at the City University of New York. She received a BA with Honors from Wesleyan University and a Ph.D. in Urban Studies from the Massachusetts Institute of Technology.

Euskadi
Bilbao, 2015

There are bubbles, scrapes, tell-tale curved planes of steel. This is not
the red   and green and white
of southern France, but an enveloping, belonging,
lack thereof.

The elderly man and woman speak patiently about their grandson.
At first, in this land, on this soil, I could not read between the lines
        of their grievances—
claims about this nation and its ancient people, *homelandias*.
                                        To be tethered to, even
in this age of supply chains,
                        export processing zones,
                                        drones.

I squint my eyes and stretch out my fingertips for the legible—
In order to hear through sight, in order to make sense through tactiles.
For antiretrovirals in prison,

for reconciliations,

                    for timeliness

rather than time. For not *nots*, for not *buts*.
The explicit demand, a constitutional mandate to be close to family,
to see them on weekends,

                 to smell the same sea,

                       touch the hardness

or softness of the same water from the running faucet.
A ceasefire in exile constitutes agoraphobic confinement, even by foot.

Each day, I see them standing, wearing heavy placards proclaiming,
Etxean Nahi Ditugu !   A space before the exclamation mark.
(Walking by in the public square, the only one without white hair.
Thinking back to Fahad's parents, who thought they could
travel to Florence to see their son. To where they could perhaps be
      separated

by glass, by skin,

             by generation,

                   less than

concrete, more than grief. Less than a screen, a phantom
of an exchange. By an exchange of feeling.)
Besides *pintxos*, a counterpunch of tears. Banishment is not only
for Agave, the internally displaced.

A dispersal is not
a diaspora but
a population-wide tearing of limbs. Seashells make amends, but
no pilgrimage atones.

Kristen Sze-Tu

Kristen Sze-Tu is the granddaughter of Cantonese immigrants. She currently lives and writes in New York City, where she also works as a bookseller and educator.

titles for my family history

a thing we all know and a thing we don't
for the yellow girl with no home
a boat becomes a metaphor
nobody has been back since
none of us speak Cantonese anymore
the old country is gone
straight teeth are for movie stars
I'm sorry I forgot
how lucky we are
we still burn paper money
a birth mother forgets the smell of her children
a son rises in the west
ho nui, ho nui
you write the story
America swallowed the pen
we forgot how to play in the floodwater
nobody wrote down the folk songs
for the next generation
true story
sometimes I don't want to be Chinese anymore
somebody gave away the cheung som
everybody still has the skin

Eileen R. Tabios

Eileen R. Tabios has released over sixty collections of poetry, fiction, essays, and experimental biographies from publishers in eleven countries and cyberspace. In Spring 2021, she released her first novel *DoveLion: A Fairy Tale for Our Times*. Her 2020 books include a short story collection, *PAGPAG: The Dictator's Aftermath in the Diaspora*; a poetry collection, *The In(ter)vention of the Hay(na)ku: Selected Tercets 1996-2019*; and her third bilingual edition (English/Thai), *INCULPATORY EVIDENCE: Covid-19 Poems*. Her award-winning body of work includes invention of the hay(na)ku, a 21st century diasporic poetic form, and the MDR Poetry Generator that can create poems totaling theoretical infinity, as well as a first poetry book, *Beyond Life Sentences*, which received the Philippines' National Book Award for Poetry. Translated into eleven languages, she also has edited, co-edited or conceptualized fifteen anthologies of poetry, fiction, and essays.

Witnessed in the Convex Mirror: The Song of Space

from The Ashbery Riff-Offs, *where each poem begins with 1 or 1-2 lines from "Self-Portrait in a Convex Mirror" by John Ashbery*

We set out to accomplish and wanted so desperately
to see come into being our corralled chords
disciplined into the sublime—it is otherwise impossible
to heighten cathedrals into a space where supplicants
will feel their smallness, thus, comprehend they are not
gods. When I was young, I railed at this attempt by
architects (usually bearded men—no surprise!) who, it
seemed to me, conspired to lock humanity on the same
terrain populated by insects—bugs whose span of
the universe logically matches the tiny scale of their
bodies. Years passed and I woke up on a bench sleeping
amidst others who'd crawled in during the night seeking

solace from the freeze outside. I opened my eyes to
a rainbow settling itself upon my chest. I looked at this
odd light and whispered, "I'm no pot of gold, dear
Parmigianino." Creaking, I sat up, looked around, then
stood to approach what called me: a massive marble
altar festooned with candles, lit and unlit, fat and
thin, and in varying stages of meltdown. I was, I admit,
also attracted to a nearby cart of free coffee with
milk. Above me, the altar, and the make-shift breakfast
loomed a stained-glass window from where sunrays
had entered then descended as a rainbow to wake
me. I looked at the window where someone's son
smiled with a love unfamiliar in the alleys familiar
to me. And in turning my gaze heavenward (as it were),
I felt again the largeness of the space created by a
cathedral that rose to meet its God. Thus, did I realize
the error of my youth: art—especially masterpieces—
elevates humanity. For no art was possible without
human ambition—that audacity and *grace*—that spares
us from the fate of our insect brothers and sisters. At
such a moment, there was nothing else to do but for me
to put down the Styrofoam cup, part my lips, raise chest
toward the hidden angels, and break into song. My chords
were disciplined. My chords were strong. I sang, and
my ambitious voice filled the massive cathedral space
into capacity. I came into being, capacious and singing

Lehua M. Taitano

Lehua M. Taitano is a queer CHamoru artist and writer from Yigo, Guåhan. She is the author of *Inside Me an Island* (Wordtech Editions, 2018) and *A Bell Made of Stones* (Tinfish Press, 2013) and is co-founder of Art 25: Art in the Twenty-fifth Century, an artist collective that investigates how Indigenous and Black art lives in the 21st century and beyond. Taitano hustles her way through the capitalist labyrinth as a bike mechanic and believes in poetry that reimagines, reconfigures, and rewrites the mapping of bodies and the Earth.

Cedar Waxwings, Pyracantha
from *A Queer Ornithology*

Once,   a shrub implored me   to press

                             my ear to the earth

     and   listen   to its thrumming

              roots.

                      It stretched toward a future

         self   and glimpsed my   intention,

                     the sickle

   arc of my eye.

           I grasped,   pricked my finger

                  on an archetype.

Most stories will say

         let the blade ring

             true.

    Ask   the   once shuddering   limbs gone
brown
     with winter   rain.

Times I am history   dumb,

                                    an ancestor   surfaces like a red glistening
                        droplet.
Otherwise a cat
                        will appear   from back of   the shed,

mewl   once   and   mist   away.

                Next autumn—   sprawl.

Branches   blaze laden   splay

                        beyond the wall,

clusters bobbing.

                                Waxwings,

            pinion   me a story.

                                Well, says one.

                                                            Listen

Islanders Waiting for Snow

The snow has not come
though our every deflation is
a chant for erasure.

Wind in our lungs we
huff, shiver its own drama,

the breath decibel one-tenth
a yelp. Concurrent, squint.

A cloud roils wing-black,
feinting puncture,
abdominal and swift.

White blanket, make
a desert of our nostalgia.

Unshouting, our desire
aches like a wedge.

Paul Tran

Paul Tran is the recipient of the Ruth Lilly & Dorothy Sargent Rosenberg Fellowship from the Poetry Foundation and the Discovery/Boston Review Poetry Prize. Their work appears in *The New Yorker*, *Poetry* Magazine, and elsewhere, including the RZA-directed movie *Love Beats Rhymes* with Azealia Banks, Common, and Jill Scott. They are the Poetry Editor at *The Offing* Magazine, which won a Whiting Literary Magazine Award from the Whiting Foundation, and a Wallace Stegner Fellow in Poetry at Stanford University.

Elegy with My Mother's Lipstick

I climb down to the beach facing the Pacific Ocean. Torrents of rain shirr the sand. On the other side, my grandmother sleeps soundlessly in her bed. Her áo dài of the whitest silk. My mother knew her mother died before the telephone rang like bells announcing the last American helicopter leaving Sài Gòn. Arrow shot back to its bow. Long-distance missile. She'd leap into the sky to fly home if she could. She works overtime instead. Curls her hair with hot rollers. Rouges her cheeks like Gong Li in Raise the Red Lantern. And I'm her understudy. Hiding in the doorway between her grief and mine, I apply her foundation to my face. I conceal the parts of me she conceals, puckering my lips as if to kiss a man that loves me the way I want to be loved. I speak their bewitching names aloud. Twisted Rose. Fuchsia in Paris.

     Irreverence.

I choose the lipstick she'd least approve. My mouth a pomegranate split open. A grenade with a loose pin. In the kitchen, I wrap a white sheet around my waist and dance for hours, mesmerized by my reflection in a charred skillet. I laugh her laugh, the way my grandmother laughed when she taught me to pray the Chú Đại Bi, when I braided her hair in unbearable heat. My tiny fingers weaving silver strands into a fishtail, a French twist. Each knot a future she never named, buried in the soil of her, where she locked away the image of her sons and daughters locked away. I'm sorry, mother of my mother, immortal bodhisattva with a thousand hands, chewing a fist of betel root, your teeth black as dawn. No child in our family stays a child their mother can love.

Scientific Method

Of course I chose the terry cloth surrogate. Milkless
artifice. False idol. Everyone, I'm told, has a mother,

but Master bred me in a laboratory, his colony
of orphans. Rhesus macaque. *Macaca mulatta*. Old
World monkeys, my matriarchs ruled the grasslands

and forests long before white men like him weaned
their whiteness and maleness from our chromosomes,

slashed and burned our home, what they once called
The Orient. French Indochina. Việt Nam. Master,
like a good despot, besotted and dumbstruck, dying

to discern the genesis of allegiance, the science of love
and loss, nature versus nurture, segregated me at birth

from my maker, pelt sopping with placental blood.
In a chamber where he kept track of me, his pupils
recorded my every movement, my every utterance,

hoping I might evince to them a part of themselves.
But I wasn't stupid. I knew famine and emaciation,

and nevertheless I picked that lifeless piece of shit
because it was soft to hold. Who wouldn't want that?
Though it couldn't hold me, I clung to the yellow-face

devil as though it was my true mother and I grasped
the function of motherhood: witness to my suffering,

companion in hell. Unlike infants with wire mothers
I didn't hurl myself on the floor in terror or tantrum,
rocking back and forth, colder than a corpse. I had

what Master believed to be a psychological base
of operations. Emotional attachment. Autonomy.

Everything he denied and did to me, his ceaseless
cruelty concealed as inquisition, unthinkable until
it was thought, I endured by keeping for myself

the wisdom he yearned to discover and take credit
for. Love, like me, is a beast no master can maim,

no dungeon can discipline. Love is at once master
and dungeon. So don't underestimate me. Simple-
minded and subservient as I might appear to be,

I gathered more about Master than he did
about me, which, I guess, is a kind of fidelity

conceived not from fondness but fear magnified
by fascination. Master made me his terry cloth
surrogate, his red-clawed god, nursing his id

on my tits, and for that, I pitied him. All this time
he was the animal. All this time he belonged to me.

Alaisha Verdeflor

Alaisha Verdeflor is a queer Filipino poet from New Jersey. Her writing explores the haunt and joy of diaspora across generations, time, and space. She is much influenced by food as a preservation of home. Currently, she is pursuing an MPH, building community, and cooking delicious pots.

Palindrome for Buko Pie
for Lola

even when memory failed us, at least that was there.
buko pie. its hardened crust encasing its slipping parts.
much of the same can be said about the body &
though we try not to admit it
time unravels towards what we already knew—
the uncalling of names, then
either I am your apo your daughter your sibling,
who we are remaining weightless in its form
we push away the need for goodbyes
let silence swallow us, tightly holding
the nearest thing that anchors us to here—
El Ideal Buko Pie, I unbox
the delicacy, an unchanging design, cut a slice of
nostalgia—how easily this becomes our routine:

> *we share this piece together*
> *sweet custard cooled into browned skin*
> *your warm smile*
> *the lines on my face*
> *how they mirror yours*
> *remember*
> *Inday, Inday*
> *it's been so long since you've been home*
> *forget*
> *retreat into another fantasy*

we allow the confusion of unknowing to settle
deeper into the moments of regret. Before
sea-thatched land turned to years lost
once, there was you & I meeting for the first time under
the slick of falling rain
from the palm trees. o, how we used to wait for
stockpiles of young coconut to /
ground into the soil, watch the hollow shells burst
with all its rich insides still intact,

Isabella Wang

Isabella Wang is an emerging, Chinese Canadian immigrant writer residing on the unceded and unsurrendered territories of the Musqueam, Squamish, and Tsleil-Waututh peoples. She is the author of *On Forgetting a Language* (Baseline Press, 2019). She has been shortlisted twice for *The New Quarterly*'s Edna Staebler Essay Contest. Her poetry and prose have appeared in over twenty literary journals including *Prairie Fire*, *The /tEmz/Review*, and *carte blanche*, and are forthcoming in three anthologies. She is pursuing a double major in English and World Literature at Simon Fraser University, while co-ordinating the bi-monthly Dead Poets Reading Series, serving as an RA for Oecologies, an RA for SpokenWeb, and an assistant editor with *Room* magazine.

Spawning Grounds

A female salmon by intuition returns to her pre-natal stream carrying the weight of up to 3,000 eggs. This, she will climb to deposit in the hollows of gravel and sediment above falls, packed between fresh-water river beds but to be met along the way by the dam on Muskrat Falls off Labrador, the Keeyask dam on the Nelson River, 93 square kilometres of hydro across boreal lands, snow forests liquefied where a common spawning ground resides for the wild fish being met with the Site C Dam though BC— 128 kilometres of river flooded, the Peace River a reservoir, an Indigenous burial ground and home to 100 endangered species. On the south, 76 killer whales left on the brink of extinction. We erect hydro dams and rear fish in hatcheries away from their natural habitat, bring wildlife back into nature, nature back into industrialization: this is what we call rewilding. The bare necessities of hatcheries strengthened through genetic engineering, forced interbreeding, but fish that rely on muscle memory year after year are the ones we see failing to return.

Kara Kai Wang

Kara Kai Wang is a Chinese American poet based in San Francisco. Her work appears or is forthcoming in *The Margins, Indiana Review, Copper Nickel,* and other journals. She has received residencies from MacDowell Colony and Vermont Studio Center. She is currently working on a manuscript that speaks to her parents' experience during the Cultural Revolution in China under Chairman Mao. A graduate of University of Oregon's MFA program, she is currently a third-year medical student at UCSF, after which she plans on specializing in psychiatry.

My mother tells me this is privilege
1969, the cult of the mango

Of miracles, Mao once declared a mango *a spiritual time bomb.*
The people of China worshipped this golden fruit, as it travelled
from province to town to the hungry hands of a small village
where a dentist remarked *How like a sweet potato!*
He was executed on the spot. No explosion, no tick tick,
just an abdomen slit open to reveal a wide-eyed boy,
cowering behind his poem of gingko and China.
The guards killed this too, his little art.
It's said when Mao first learned his people were starving
he stopped eating meat. Paced the long soil halls
of his estate and composed poems of sorrow,
3 years and 30 million dead. I do not envy the birds
he wrung into metaphors. If he wandered lonely
as a cloud, my mother wandered not at all.
Have you heard her persimmons at dusk?
In the childhood I have combed with a fine-haired girl,
they have always been a kind of heaven. Plump fruit blooming
beneath a bitter skin, bloodied with song—*how like a tongue!*

the execution of 小金

1968, Communist China

every time I imagine her   I see Shanghai burning

     the flames engulfing the city in a gaping mouth
of crimson peonies, abandoned spoons

and the upturned legs of breakfast chairs

I imagine the older children fleeing
     down stairs to witness the fire

     their mothers pocketing the month's last rations
two purple plums, a pouch of rice
and a chicken egg too precious to eat or sell

in the street
     小金, a schoolteacher kneels

     her hands are silver basins pooling with river water

even on her knees she is defiant

     her spine a white bone arrow
          taut beneath the heavens

the fire divides as the crowd jeers

     dressed in red, a man runs forward and hurls a wooden plank
against the soft nape of her neck

     小金 crumples

and the neighborhood children, no longer

        under her gaze, scramble forward to beat
the broken wood against her back

her hair a black swan weeping on the stones

filthy they chant *spy*
    they chant

the fire roars and the children scramble back,
joining the crowd

    of hungry crows, aglow in the red

red light

       of revolution

—

小金

tonight I dream an army of silkworms

descend from the mulberry leaves of Shanghai

their plumes of silk turn mid-air into filaments

of light, a new moon bathed in old land

"Struggle sessions" were a form of public humiliation that was commonly used during the Cultural Revolution of China as a tool to instill fear in the public and humiliate individuals who were deemed a threat to the Communist Party. They were typically conducted in front of the community, where the accused person would be forced to admit their treason to the Chinese government, and the crowds would verbally and often physically abuse the accused person.

Maw Shein Win

Maw Shein Win is a poet, editor, and educator who lives and teaches in the Bay Area. Her poetry chapbooks are *Ruins of a glittering palace* (SPA/Commonwealth Projects, 2013) and *Score and Bone* (Nomadic Press, 2016). *Invisible Gifts: Poems* was published by Manic D Press in 2018. She was a 2019 Visiting Scholar in the Department of English at UC Berkeley. Win is the first poet laureate of El Cerrito, California (2016 - 2018). Her full-length poetry collection is *Storage Unit for the Spirit House* (Omnidawn, 2020), longlisted for the 2021 PEN America Open Book Award. She often collaborates with visual artists, musicians, and other writers and is a Spring 2021 ARC Poetry Fellow at UC Berkeley.

Spirit House (one)

the *nats* have stolen my hair

mosquito net winds itself around limbs

watch clumps of black hair blow across the room onto balcony

the house on Inya Lake presses down on my neck & back

smell of jackfruit & sweet orange consoles me

eat semolina cake under crackling palms

hear the cousins gossip: *she is so idle, not as enterprising as her four sisters*

sometimes I cannot bear to watch these sunsets

Note: A *nat* is a Burmese animist deity.

Annette Wong

Annette Wong is a Chinese American writer, lawyer, and meditation teacher. She is currently an MFA candidate at Warren Wilson College, where she was the 2019-2020 Rona Jaffe Foundation Graduate Fellow in Creative Writing. Her poems grapple with language, family, and loss. Her poems have appeared in *Waxwing*, *Poetry Northwest*, and *Lantern Review*. Annette holds a BA from Yale University and a JD from the University of Southern California. Her work has benefited from the support of teachers and friends from the Bread Loaf Writers' Conference, the AWP Writer-to-Writer Mentorship Program, the Community of Writers in Squaw Valley, VONA, Writing Workshops Los Angeles, and her Daily Grind group.

Tuol Sleng

When the power went,
there had been rain for five days,
scattering the hawkers, the *motos,*
the men sprawled in their *tuktuks.*
Ants flecked the rambutan
plucked from a wet market
stall, days shy of ripe.

I live behind the Genocide Museum. I wrote home.
It sounds grimmer than it is.

It wasn't the spattered tiles
that got to me most,
or the whites of eyes captured
on camera, the metal beds
on which bodies were strung—but the thought—
of each prisoner's last glimpse

of sun, ruptured, through the shutters
and perforated walls
before the blindfolds, the transport,
fifteen kilometers to *Choeung Ek*,
the Killing Fields, where speakers hung
from The Magic Tree blaring:

Children, do not forget the fresh blood of our soldiers and
Children, forever remember the revolution!

Now, darkness. New sounds audible,
without the percussive rain and hum of motors:
ceramic on tin, the neighbors' dinner utensils
set to rest. In the alley, children
with candles, laughing. The patter of hands
on smooth surfaces, the collective search
for something to light.

Tuol Sleung, also known as Security Prison (S-21), was a former high school in Phnom Penh, Cambodia, which the Khmer Rouge turned into an execution center. Prisoners who were not killed at S-21 were transported to the Killing Fields for execution. It is now a Genocide Museum.

The Magic Tree is a tree in the *Choeung Ek* killing fields upon which the Khmer Rouge strung loudspeakers that played propaganda and music as victims were being executed.

On Reciting Li Bai

(to the Community of Writers)

I don't pretend to understand
Tang poetry. I learned the poems

from my mother, as a girl, and just a few—
tools for learning Mandarin (and behavioral control)—

the one about the farmer
tilling the land, each grain of rice

in my bowl, a bead of sweat
(so I would finish my food),

the one about the mother, *Song of the Wanderer*
number 45 of *300 Tang Poems*,

stitching her wayward son's clothes,
(to highlight a mother's worry and care).

And yes, the one about the scholar
looking at the moon, thinking of home,

to say, *remember who you are* (and here I am,
translating again, in the loosest sense,

my literary Chinese, a semester in college),
which I, last night, bolstered by wine,

and the desire to fill this space
with a voice like mine,

like hers,
shared.

Jane Wong

Jane Wong is a Chinese American poet born and raised on the Jersey shore. Her poems can be found in places such as *POETRY, American Poetry Review, AGNI, Third Coast,* and other journals. A Kundiman fellow and Pushcart Prize recipient, she is the author of *Overpour* (Action Books, 2016) and *How to Not Be Afraid of Everything* (Alice James Books, 2021). She is an Associate Professor of Creative Writing at Western Washington University. Inspired by Marilyn Chin, she considers herself a "wild girl poet." In *The Margins,* Wong writes: "It's about resistance, about taking risks, about matrilineal and literary lineage, about laughter, about not being afraid of being too loud or too quiet. About listening closely to what rustles under the ice. About cultivating your own power and the power of the people you love deeply."

Lessons on Lessening

I wake to the sound of my neighbors upstairs as if they are bowling.

And maybe they are, all pins and love fallen over.
I lay against my floor, if only to feel that kind of affection.

What I've learned, time and again:
Get up. You can not have what they have.

And the eyes of a dead rat can't say anything.

In Jersey, the sink breaks and my mother keeps a bucket
underneath to save water for laundry.

A trickle of water is no joke. I've learned that.
Neither is my father, wielding a knife in starlight.

I was taught that everything and everyone is self-made.

That you can make a window out of anything if you want.
This is why I froze insects. To see if they will come back to life.

How I began to see each day: the sluice of wings.
Get up. The ants pouring out of the sink, onto my arms in dish-heavy
      water.

My arms: branches. A swarm I didn't ask for.

No one told me I'd have to learn to be polite.
To let myself be consumed for what I can not control.

I must return to my younger self. To wearing my life
like heavy wool, weaved in my own weight.

To pretend not to know when the debtors come to collect.

Nellie Wong

Oakland Chinatown-born, Nellie Wong has published four books: *Dreams in Harrison Railroad Park* (Kelsey Street Press, 1977), *The Death of Long Steam Lady* (West End Press, 1986), *Stolen Moments* (Chicory Blue Press, 1987), and *Breakfast Lunch Dinner* (Meridien PressWorks, 2012). Her poems and essays appear in numerous journals and anthologies, and two pieces are installed at public sites in San Francisco. She is co-featured in the documentary film, *Mitsuye and Nellie: Asian American Poets*, and among her recognitions is a building at Oakland High School named after her. She traveled to China in the First American Women Writers Tour with Alice Walker, Tillie Olsen, and Paule Marshall, among others.

While You Are Alive?

While you are still dreaming?
While you examine the orange protea's majesty?
While you walk 10,000 steps daily?
While you await cataract surgery?
While you put coins in a black man's empty paper cup?
While you watch a two-year-old boy hug a stranger, another
      two-year-old boy?
While you shake your head at food spilling out of a shoe box at the
      bus stop?
While you fill your calendar with doctors' appointments?
While you soak dried bean curd for salad and soup?
While you still remember how to write in shorthand?
While you empty the compost bin?
While you hum the melody of a love song not understanding Mandarin?
While you visit Eric, homeless, handsome in a new windbreaker?
While you stand for open borders?

While you defend women's right to choose?
While you start writing cinquains?
While you smile at four noisy baby girls on the bus?
While you no longer drive?
While you upright a rubber toy dinosaur lying on the street?
While you lift a thousand pounds of feathers?
While you are alive?

Shelley Wong

Shelley Wong is a queer, fourth-generation Chinese American poet from Long Beach, California, who currently lives in San Francisco. She is the author of *As She Appears* (YesYes Books, 2022), winner of the 2019 Pamet River Prize, and the chapbook *RARE BIRDS* (Diode Editions, 2017). Her poems have appeared in *American Poetry Review*, *Best American Poetry 2021*, *Kenyon Review*, and *The New Republic*. She is an affiliate artist at Headlands Center for the Arts and the recipient of a Pushcart Prize, along with fellowships from Kundiman, MacDowell, and Vermont Studio Center. She is interested in radical beauty and queer femme abundance.

[the ocean will take us one day]

My first memory is when the tide pulled me

into its room. On land, my mistake as an adult
was letting the laws go by, unannounced.

When you enter a city, check the elevation

on the welcome sign. This month, the moon
was as close as it will ever be

in our lifetime. This month, the police

let the drowning loose.
The tide may be tired, but never tires.

Was it worth it, what you did

to live by the sea? Stay with me
in bare light, undone. In recovery,

two states drift toward one another

and repel, like soldiers. Rapture,
I've felt that, too. Who will stop a man

from having his way? I go under

to drag the words out of the deep.
The women were brave and beautiful.

The women were brave and beautiful their entire lives.

All Beyoncés & Lucy Lius

where are you from / the LBC / can you speak / har gow siu mai /
June Lena Rose & Waverly / black tea with boba 50% ice 75% sweetness / baked or steamed bao / area code 415 vs 510 / don't trust banh
mi over $5 / Richmond or Richmond District / what do your peo-
ple call jook / eight is lucky in Chinese because it sounds like luck /
why didn't Jet Li kiss Aaliyah / what is the best late-night restaurant in
Chinatown / *The Woman Warrior* is canon / little girls in pink & red
/ Angel Island poetry / the 80 freeway to 880 to 580 to 980 to 680 to
780 / in Berkeley they are quick with the ma'am / four is bad luck / I
can't tell Mandarin from Cantonese / incense altars with oranges / is
she hapa / Buddha raising money above his head / the 5 to the 405 to
the 605 to the 10 to the 101 / Lucy Liu & my girl Drew / Cameron D
& Destiny / if I dress in all black I can take control / monolid makeup
tips on YouTube / Maggie Cheung / small ceramic white cat with one
raised paw / mixed meat with pan-fried noodles / the 110 to the 105
to the 710 to the 91 / Hello Kitty Little Twin Stars My Melody / I

calculate my proportions with finesse / like a G6 like a G6 / that Joy Luck Club watermelon scene / in Hong Kong people look like my relatives / Cameron D went to my high school / Wong Kar-Wai films will break your heart / Burmese tea leaf salad / older folks doing t'ai chi by the BART station / Keanu Reeves is part Chinese / in Hawaiian his name means "cool breeze over the mountains" / 213 vs 310 vs 562 / I would sincerely rock a cheongsam / Cibo Matto is playing at the Bronze tonight / a dog named Panda / get up Jeremy Lin we love you / don't trust a pho place without a number in its name / turkey jook after Thanksgiving / yellow Power Ranger / Claudia Kishi / James Iha / Better Luck Tomorrow / Michelle Kwan was robbed in the 98 Olympics / she is divorced & practicing at her ice rink / Fields of Gold forever / Mulan against the world / Chinese love cash

Jessica Yuan

Jessica Yuan is a Chinese American poet and designer, born and raised in southern California as a second generation immigrant. Her work is deeply influenced by heritage and themes of alienation and mistranslation, not only between languages, but also between personal and national history and between experience and nostalgia. She is the author of the chapbook *Threshold Amnesia*, winner of the Yemassee Chapbook Contest. Jessica has received fellowships from Kundiman and Miami Writer's Institute, and has published poems in *jubilat, The Southampton Review, The Journal, Boulevard,* and elsewhere. She is currently based in Boston, where she is a Masters of Architecture candidate at Harvard.

American tourist

my father in the living room watches alaska: the last frontier.
he tells me, my grandmother's sheep were never trimmed

around the eyes, they could be sat on (they listened to everything.)
each episode, a barnyard animal is eaten, made much of.

on the bus ride to yellowstone we spoke more of homeland
than the plains moving past us or the things

we came to see (like freedom and history and greatness.)
by the roadside boy scouts stopped and stared, wading through meadows

for old antlers. I would read little house on the prairie to my mother
who is so like them (full of quilts and survival,)

she would tell me so much about hunger I never believed
it was something I'd felt. my father likes silence and the past.

he votes for losing candidates (he is so unwilling to love charismatic
        men.)
he believes in the things we are given, like decency.

we cross the hoover dam and he is proud of it all. not history,
but being here. not the things that went wrong

but that they are built. the pasture you find on stolen land
like extending a hand into an unlit room.

we sit on a cruise boat in summer and face a glacier near juneau.
the towns have wood sidewalks and I am photographed with men

holding axes, the lands they ravaged, the hair on their arms.
my father tells me about leaving the farm and I see cabin,

warm eggs, soft dirt and it fading. This is how you invent
a home, burying myth after myth at the edges, a line

of my people filing one by one to stare
at a beautiful nation.

Jihyun Yun

Jihyun Yun is a Korean American poet from the Bay Area in California. A Fulbright Research fellow, she received her BA from UC Davis and her MFA from New York University. She is the author of the Prairie Schooner Prize winning collection *Some Are Always Hungry* (University of Nebraska Press, 2020). Her poetry catalogues her family's history during the Korean War and subsequent immigration to the United States through the lens of food or the lack thereof. Her poems can be found in *Narrative Magazine*, *Bat City Review*, *Best New Poets*, and elsewhere.

All Female

At the night-markets, women
peddle their prices, shout in swift
Cantonese over gurgling tanks
of sea spawn: snails, young eels born
for smoke, coal, skewers. The blood
clams loll, tongues over shell lips
as we buy a bag of cockles
and three crabs, sweet with egg.
Their claws beg, puncture holes
in the cherry red, *Please come again.*

At home, my women crack them open,
cleaver at lip's hem, plunge and snap.
The men watch game shows,
as we wreck the girl bodies
for roe, and I don't know why.

They are always sweeter, more pricey,
Halmeoni says, pulling the last claw

from the last crab, stumps still writhing
in the sink. She dismantles the breast next
and what pulsates inside is all gully and wet.

It's always the girls, for everything.
When was the last time you've heard
of a rooster soup? We put the bodies
to boil in salt and broth.

Outside, the winter
interrogates, our windows
fogged, and in our bodies
we are always lost.

If our feast ever happens,
if time has not misplaced us,
may these girls rise violet
from the pot, untangle their legs
from perilla and leek
and make for the sea
with their limbs in their teeth.

The Wives

For L.B.N

"The wolves wore woman faces. I was always afraid. My father was tex-
tile rich with many wives. My mother, the youngest of them, was the
only one God sent a son through. I was the prize mother's cheek was
ground on washboards for, pulped mess I bloodied my mouth on to
prove how she was loved. The wives descended at night with all their
teeth. I hid behind the paper screen, watched shadows beat shadow
in the lamplight's flex & release. Then the animal shit left at our door
before dawn. Then the suppers laced with wisteria which we ate &

198

heaved like dogs. I dreamt of leaving and I left. The impossible milk of morning made me run away. I kicked dust in the occupied streets as kids cupped their hands in hunger, struggled with the weight of my tongue, dodged Japanese night patrol until I couldn't, was brought back cut & gaunt. *No son of mine would bring me this shame. Both the bitch & the whelp have rotted.* Fallen from favor, mother held to father's knees saying 'we will not go, we will not go,' for what did we know of hunger? The wolves smothered their laughs, gathered around in their gowns of dyed silk. The night sky we stood under pulsed like something hurting."

Acknowledgements

Some of the poems in *They Rise Like A Wave* have appeared in other magazines, chapbooks, and online websites. We gratefully acknowledge those publications, their editors, and staff.

JESSICA ABUGHATTAS, "The Wedding" originally appeared in *Stirring Lit*. "Merci" originally appeared in *Rogue Agent Journal*. MARCI CALABRETTA CANCIO-BELLO, "In the Animal Garden of My Body" appeared on the Academy of American Poets *Poem-a-Day*. CATHERINE CHEN, "There Is No Body of a Poem" originally appeared in *GlitterMob*. "When the ice is at last" originally appeared in *bæst journal*. JENNIFER S. CHENG, "Letters to Mao" originally appeared in *House A*, (Omnidawn, 2016). "Biography of Women in the Sea" originally appeared in *MOON: Letters, Maps, Poems*, (Tarpaulin Sky, 2018). SU CHO, "Tangerine Trees & Little Bags of Thrush" originally appeared in the *Poetry Journal*, online. "The Old Man in White Has Given My Mother a Ripe Persimmon" originally appeared in *Pleiades*. FRANNY CHOI, "Turing Test" originally appeared in *Soft Science*, (Alice James Books, 2019). "Cloven" originally appeared in *American Poetry Review*. CARLINA DUAN, "Alien Miss at the Immigration Station" originally appeared in the *Michigan Quarterly Review* under the title "Angel Island." ANUJA GHIMIRE, "A humanitarian walks into a village in Nepal" originally appeared in *Glass: a journal of poetry*. DENA IGUSTI, "after the incision" originally appeared in *The Shanghai Literary Review*. ANN INOSHITA, "Japan Trip" originally appeared in *Manoa Stream* (Kahuaomānoa Press, 2007). DOYALI ISLAM, "light" originally appeared in *heft*, (McClelland & Stewart, 2019). MADDIE KIM, "Letter to My Ancestors" originally appeared in *Tinderbox Poetry Journal*; "How I Wait for You to Return from Your Naturalization Ceremony" originally appeared in *The Margins*. HYEJUNG KOOK, "The Day Dr. Christine Blasey Ford Testifies" originally appeared in *Glass: A Journal of Poetry* Poets Resist 2018 Midterm Elections Special Feature. IRIS

A. LAW, "Cut Pieces" originally appeared in *Dusie*. JENNA LE, "Purses" originally appeared in *Literary Matters*. "Epicenter Thoughts" originally appeared in *MiGoZine*. KAREN AN-HWEI LEE, "On the Levitation of Beautiful Objects" originally appeared in *Prairie Schooner*. MARI L'ESPERANCE, "Anju, from the Far World" originally appeared in *Hoppenthaler's Congeries at Connotation Press: Online*. NANCY CHEN LONG, "Why There Is No Interest in Singing" originally appeared in *The Adroit Journal*. MIA AYUMI MALHOTRA, "Notes from the Birth Year: on Worlds" originally appeared in *The Yale Review Online*. "Toward an Unfinished Work III" originally appeared in *A Bad Penny Review*. AURORA MASUM-JAVED, "Fine Lines" originally appeared in *Winter Tangerine*. "After three cups of kava, I name every good thing I never asked for" originally appeared in the *Nimrod International Journal of Prose and Poetry*. DIANA KHOI NGUYEN, "A Story about Holes" originally appeared in *The Kweli Journal*. ALYSSA OGI, "Tree Haibun" originally appeared in the *Best New Poets 2017 Anthology*. YAMINI PATHAK, "Ahimsa" originally appeared in *Waxwing*. MICHELLE PEÑALOZA, "Post Diaspora" originally appeared in *Prairie Schooner*. MEGAN PINTO, "To the Old Man Who Lived on a Hill" originally appeared in *Ploughshares*. PREETI KAUR RAJPAL, "watching the wagah border closing ceremony" originally appeared in *Blueshift Journal*. SWATI RANA, "Plane Ride after 9/11" originally appeared in *Salt 2*. KAREN RIGBY, "After a Line by Montaigne" originally appeared in *Palette Poetry*. C.E. SHUE, "How to Bind a Book of Fortunes" numbered lines are instructions collected from *Unique Handmade Books* by Alisa Golden, (Sterling Publishing Company, Inc. 2003). KRISTEN SZE-TU, "titles for my family history" originally appeared in *Winter Tangerine*. EILEEN R. TABIOS, "Witnessed in the Convex Mirror: The Song of Space" originally appeared in *Berfrois*. LEHUA M. TAITANO, "Cedar Waxwings, Pyracantha" originally appeared in the *Tayo Literary Magazine*. "Islanders Waiting for Snow" originally appeared in *Inside Me an Island* (WordTech Editions, 2018). PAUL TRAN, "Elegy with My Mother's Lipstick" originally appeared in *The Boiler*. "Scientific Method" originally appeared in *Poetry*.

ANNETTE WONG, "Tuol Sleng" a version of this poem originally appeared in the *Altadena Poetry Review*. SHELLY WONG, "[the ocean will take us one day]" and "All Beyoncés & Lucy Lius" originally appeared in the *Kenyon Review Online*. JESSICA YUAN, "American Tourist" originally appeared in *The Margins*. JIHYUN YUN, "All Female" originally appeared in *Narrative Magazine*. "The Wives" originally appeared in *Muse/A*.

Thanks To

Garrett Hongo, who suggested that both Christine Kitano and Alycia Pirmohamed would make outstanding editors of this anthology. Their keen choices of poets and poems resound throughout the anthology. Thanks to Joshua McKinney for his sharp editorial eye and advice; to Jane Hirschfield, who warned me of the literary trials in creating an anthology; to Rhony Bhopla who early on had great suggestions; and to Pos Moua whose presence we all miss. The success of the Blue Oak Press publication of his *Karst Mountains Will Bloom* (2019) provided the means to publish *They Rise Like A Wave*. Thank you also to Sandra McPherson for her wisdom, advice, and encouragement; to Jennifer Wu for her gift of the cover photograph to this project; to the kind folks at the Sacramento Viewpoint Gallery; to Maxima Kahn and her cover design magic; to BOP webpage designer Carmela Yeseta; to Blue Oak Press interns Michaela Erwin and Quynh Tran; to my Asian American neighbors, students, and friends who helped me see the world anew; and finally to Okei Ito whose life and legacy here in the Sierra Nevada foothills as part of the Wakamatsu Tea Colony inspired me when I was a teenager.

About the Editors

Christine Kitano is the author of the poetry collections *Sky Country* and *Birds of Paradise*, and co-author of the oral history collection *Who You: The Issei*. She is an associate professor at Ithaca College where she teaches courses in poetry and Asian American literature. She also teaches in the MFA Program for Writers at Warren Wilson College.

Alycia Pirmohamed has studied creative writing at the University of Oregon and the University of Edinburgh. She is the author of the collection *Another Way to Split Water*, and the chapbooks *Hinge*, *Faces that Fled the Wind*, and co-author with Pratyusha of *Second Memory*. Her awards include a Pushcart Prize, the Gulf Coast Poetry Contest, the CBC Poetry Prize, the 92Y Discovery Contest, and the Ploughshares Emerging Writer's Award. Alycia is also the co-founder of the Scottish BAME Writers Network and a co-organizer of the Ledbury Poetry Critics Programme. In 2020, she received the Edwin Morgan Poetry Award.

Sandeep Parmar was raised in Southern California and later earned an MA from the University of East Anglia and a PhD from University College London. She is the author of the poetry collections *The Marble Orchard* (2012) and *Eidolon* (2017), which won a Ledbury Forte Prize. With James Byrne, she collaborated on the chapbook *Myth of the Savage Tribes, Myth of Civilised Nations* (2014). *Threads*, a collaborative pamphlet with Nisha Ramayya and Bhanu Kapil, was published by Clinic in 2018. Parmar's scholarship focuses on British and American Modernism, particularly women's autobiographical writing by lesser-known writers such as Hope Mirrlees, Nancy Cunard, and Mina Loy.

Copy Editor Joshua McKinney is the author of four books of poetry most recently *Small Sillion* (Parlor Press, 2019). His work has appeared in such journals as *Boulevard*, *Denver Quarterly*, *Kenyon Review*,

New American Writing, and many others. He is the recipient of The Dorothy Brunsman Poetry Prize, The Dickinson Prize, The Pavement Saw Chapbook Prize, and a Gertrude Stein Award for Innovative Writing. He teaches literature and creative writing at California State University, Sacramento.

Randy White is the publisher and managing editor of Blue Oak Press. Besides conceiving the idea of the anthology, *They Rise Like A Wave: An Anthology of Asian American Women Poets,* he is also the author of *Motherlode/La Veta Madre* (1977), and *Blood Transparencies* (2016). His epic poem, American Mahabharata will be published in 2023.